The International Law of Peacebuilding

This book contributes to the debate on the international law of post-conflict peacebuilding and suggests a need for closer connections between practitioners and lawyers.

The work argues that significant benefits accrue when lawyers and conflict/peace practitioners, and scholars work with each other to develop a normative framework for building peace. It also attempts to bridge the divisions that exist between lawyers and the conflict resolution/peace community in the specific context of the international law of post-conflict peacebuilding. After introducing the key concepts of the international law of peacebuilding, the book explores aspects of the relationship between lawyers and peacebuilding practitioners and offers ideas about how this relationship might be improved. It then proceeds to identify some principles and processes developed by conflict resolution specialists that may inform and influence discrete parts of the international law of peacebuilding. The work concludes by identifying sites and ways in which international lawyers and conflict resolution/peace specialists may engage with each other to shape this branch of international law.

This book will be of much interest to students of peace and conflict studies, international law and International Relations.

Omar Grech is an associate professor within the Department of International Law, University of Malta and is the author of *Human Rights and the Northern Ireland Conflict: Law, Politics and Conflict, 1921–2014* (2017).

Studies in Conflict, Development and Peacebuilding

Series Editors: Keith Krause, Oliver Jütersonke and Riccardo Bocco, *Centre on Conflict, Development and Peacebuilding (CCDP), Graduate Institute, Switzerland*

This series publishes innovative research into the connections between insecurity and under-development in fragile states, and into situations of violence and insecurity more generally. It adopts a multidisciplinary approach to the study of a variety of issues, including the changing nature of contemporary armed violence (*conflict*), efforts to foster the conditions that prevent the outbreak or recurrence of such violence (*development*), and strategies to promote peaceful relations on the communal, societal and international level (*peacebuilding*).

Exploring Peace Formation
Security and Justice in Post-Colonial States
Edited by Kwesi Aning, M. Anne Brown, Volker Boege, and Charles T. Hunt

Urban Safety and Peacebuilding
New Perspectives on Sustaining Peace in the City
Edited by Edited by Achim Wennmann and Oliver Jütersonke

New Paths and Policies towards Conflict Prevention
Chinese and Swiss Perspectives
Edited by Courtney J. Fung, Björn Gehrmann, Rachel F. Madenyika, and Jason G. Tower

The Political Economy of Civil War and UN Peace Operations
Edited by Mats Berdal and Jake Sherman

The International Law of Peacebuilding
Engaging the Conflict Resolution and Peace Community
Omar Grech

For more information about this series, please visit: https://www.routledge.com/Studies-in-Conflict-Development-and-Peacebuilding/book-series/CONDEVPEACE

The International Law of Peacebuilding

Engaging the Conflict Resolution and Peace Community

Omar Grech

LONDON AND NEW YORK

First published 2025
by Routledge
4 Park Square, Milton Park, Abingdon, Oxon OX14 4RN

and by Routledge
605 Third Avenue, New York, NY 10158

Routledge is an imprint of the Taylor & Francis Group, an informa business

British Library Cataloguing-in-Publication Data
A catalogue record for this book is available from the British Library

Library of Congress Cataloging-in-Publication Data
Names: Grech, Omar, author.
Title: The international law of peacebuilding : engaging the conflict resolution and peace community / Omar Grech.
Description: Abingdon, Oxon [UK] ; New York, NY : Routledge, 2025. | Series: Conflict, development and peacebuilding | Includes bibliographical references and index. | Summary: "This book contributes to the debate on the international law of post-conflict peacebuilding, and suggests a need for closer connections between practitioners and academics. The work argues that significant benefits accrue when lawyers and conflict/peace practitioners, and scholars work with each other to develop a normative framework for building peace. It also attempts to bridge the divisions that exist between lawyers and the conflict resolution/peace community in the specific context of the international law of post-conflict peacebuilding. After introducing the key concepts of the international law of peacebuilding, the book explores aspects of the relationship between lawyers and peacebuilding practitioners and offers ideas about how this relationship might be improved. It then proceeds to identify some principles and processes developed by conflict resolution specialists that may inform and influence discrete parts of the international law of peacebuilding. The work concludes by identifying sites and ways in which international lawyers and conflict resolution/peace specialists may engage with each other to shape this branch of international law. This book will be of much interest to students of peace and conflict studies, international law and International Relations"-- Provided by publisher.
Identifiers: LCCN 2024042460 (print) | LCCN 2024042461 (ebook) | ISBN 9781032611501 (hardback) | ISBN 9781032611518 (paperback) | ISBN 9781003462248 (ebook)
Subjects: LCSH: Peace-building--Law and legislation. | Postwar reconstruction.
Classification: LCC KZ6787 .G74 2025 (print) | LCC KZ6787 (ebook) | DDC 341.5/2--dc23/eng/20240913
LC record available at https://lccn.loc.gov/2024042460
LC ebook record available at https://lccn.loc.gov/2024042461

ISBN: 9781032611501 (hbk)
ISBN: 9781032611518 (pbk)
ISBN: 9781003462248 (ebk)

DOI: 10.4324/9781003462248

Typeset in Times New Roman
by KnowledgeWorks Global Ltd.

Contents

Preface

The relationship between international law and armed conflict is both ancient and profound. The first ever treaties we have a record of, are in fact, peace treaties. Among the most widely ratified treaties are the seminal Geneva Conventions of 1949, which regulate the conduct of armed conflict. The contemporary rules of international law relating to the use of armed force, both as to when it can be resorted to and how it can be conducted, have been clear since the 1940s.

The Preamble of the Charter of the United Nations, perhaps the most well-known treaty ever concluded, clarifies that its main aim is to maintain peace and avoid war. By contrast, the relationship between international law and post-conflict peacebuilding is relatively new and by and large underdeveloped.

The scholarly exploration and examination of the international law of post-conflict peacebuilding has gained sustained traction over the past decade. Nevertheless, it remains more the case that the international law of peacebuilding is a desirable objective rather than a fully fledged achievement. In legal jargon, it is more *lex ferenda* (the law as it ought to be) rather than *lex lata* (the law as it is). Suffice it to say that one cannot point to a distinct legal text, such as a treaty, which contains the essential components of the international law of peacebuilding. There remains the vexed question of what it should include and even the precise temporal contexts in which it should operate. It has been suggested that "*jus post bellum* needs to be made as strong – and as well-considered, rule-focused, and well-developed, as the other two well-defined categories of *jus ad bellum* and *jus in bello*".[1]

This book is an addition to the debate on the international law of post-conflict peacebuilding. It attempts to suggest the need for closer connections between two disciplines: international law and conflict/peace studies. As a lawyer and law lecturer, who has for a number of years worked with diplomats, conflict resolution scholars and peace practitioners, I am well aware of the mutual diffidence that exists between the various actors. I have noted that, often, postgraduate students of conflict resolution and peace studies have little or no familiarity with the basic principles of international law. Equally, international law students (as well as large sections of its community of scholars and practitioners) often have no familiarity with the principles of conflict resolution. Simultaneously, I am also aware of the mutual benefit that may occur when lawyers and conflict/peace practitioners and scholars work with each other.

This book is also an attempt to bridge some of the gaps that exist between lawyers and conflict resolution and peacebuilding (CRP) practitioners and scholars in the specific context of the international law of post-conflict peacebuilding. Given that this is a branch of international law, which is still in the process of formation and lacks codification, it seems an ideal context for engagement between lawyers and CRP practitioners and scholars.

While it is likely that disagreements between the two communities on certain issues will remain, a more cooperative framework is surely desirable. It would benefit the quality of the international law of post-conflict peacebuilding by recognising more acutely the limitations which peacebuilders face on the ground, and thus craft norms which are principled but also pragmatic.

Accordingly, the purpose of this book is thus twofold: (i) to present the emerging international law of post-conflict peacebuilding to CRP practitioners[2] and scholars as an area where they would benefit from engaging with lawyers and (ii) to encourage legal scholars who have been most active in the development of the international law of peacebuilding to engage more with those actors who are closely involved in delivering peace on the ground in post-conflict scenarios. The presentation of the basic principles of the international law of post-conflict peacebuilding in terms that are – hopefully – readily comprehensible to non-lawyers is a further objective of this book.

The book will commence with an introduction that will suggest an initial working definition of the international law of post-conflict peacebuilding as a body of norms that may assist in the transition from armed conflict to a just and sustainable peace. The Introduction will also highlight how the creation of international law has often been shaped by different non-state actors and that as an emerging field of international law of peacebuilding would benefit from the contribution of conflict resolution/peace scholars and partitioners. This will be followed by a more detailed examination of the current state of play in the development of the international law of peacebuilding, which will in itself highlight the general absence of conflict resolution/peace practitioners and scholars from the debate. Some reasons for a general lack of interaction between the international law community and the conflict resolution/peace community will then be offered. The book will then focus on the voices from the conflict resolution/peacebuilding communities in the international law of peacebuilding and suggest some of the ways in which they may be involved in shaping the development of this branch of international law. The question asked in this context is: What are the views of the CRP community that may help shape the international law of peacebuilding?

The concluding chapter will argue that is time to reset the relationship between the international legal scholars and practitioners and their CRP counterparts. In particular, the key message of this book will be reiterated: that deeper dialogue and greater cooperation in shaping the international law of peacebuilding is both an important end in itself but also a useful means to enhance the relationship between the legal community and the CRP community.

Notes

1 Stahn, C., Easterday, J. S. and Iverson, J. (2014). *Jus Post Bellum: Mapping the Normative Functions*. Oxford: Oxford University Press.

2 The term "conflict resolution/peace practitioners" refers to persons involved in the design/implementation/facilitation of conflict resolution and peacebuilding efforts in a situation of armed conflict.

Acknowledgements

This book is a result of 15 years of experience as an international law lecturer in engaging with academic colleagues at the Jimmy and Rosalynn Carter School of Peace and Conflict Resolution, United States, as well as with the students who have pursued the joint MA degree in Conflict Resolution offered by the Carter School and the University of Malta.

The conversations I had with colleagues and students have led me to develop a – hopefully – better understanding of how international law intersects with the field of conflict resolution and peacebuilding (CRP). Principally, I learned that international law is not seen as a central component of the CRP field and that the theory and practice of international law – as it relates to peacebuilding – would be improved by a greater engagement with the insights developed by the CRP community. I am genuinely thankful to all the students and colleagues who, in various ways, helped me clarify my thinking on these issues.

A special note of thanks to Professor Richard Rubenstein, Professor Emeritus of Conflict Resolution at the Carter School, who encouraged me to transform my original idea of writing an article on this subject into the rather different proposition of writing a book. His encouragement over the past 15 years has never dimmed. I am equally grateful to him for reviewing and commenting on a number of the chapters. My appreciation is also due to Professor Brice Dickson, Professor Alpaslan Ozerdem, Professor Susan Hirsch, Professor Karina Korostelina and Professor Julie Shedd, with whom I had many insightful conversations.

I am particularly grateful to all the individuals who agreed to be interviewed for the purposes of this book. In this regard, I am indebted to Ms Nina Seremet and Ms Snjezana Ivandić-Ninković, as well as Professor Constantinos Adamides, who helped me set up interviews in Bosnia Herzegovina and Cyprus, respectively.

My thanks to Dr Tony Axisa and Ms Kristina Marie Vella who helped, in various ways, to finalise the manuscript. Finally, I am pleased to record my appreciation for the encouragement and support provided by Andrew Humphrys and Max Gethings at Routledge. Andrew's support was instrumental in bringing my initial idea to fruition.

1 The International Law of Peacebuilding

An Introduction

This book rests on a key hypothesis, namely, that the quest for framing and codification of an international law of post-conflict peacebuilding has, to a large extent, been promoted by lawyers with limited engagement of conflict resolution and peace practitioners. A greater engagement of conflict resolution and peace practitioners in the process of international lawmaking requires that the essentials of international law generally and of the international law of peacebuilding particularly, be clear to them.

This chapter identifies and analyses the main elements which require clarification and lie at the heart of this hypothesis:

1 What is the relationship between international law, armed conflict and peace?
2 What are the processes through which norms of international law are codified?
3 What are the main constituent elements of the international law of peacebuilding?

This introduction will attempt to provide succinct answers to these questions. Given that these questions are amenable to voluminous commentary, the answers will necessarily be limited to the essentials which enable non-lawyers to engage with the questions being discussed.

This chapter commences by stating the problem that is addressed in the book. It then proceeds with a discussion on who creates and nourishes the interest required to cause international law norms to be codified and promoted. In this chapter, the role that may be played by both events and actors in the codification of international law is highlighted. Within this context, the role that may be played by non-state actors in this process becomes apparent. The introduction to the "process" of international lawmaking is followed by a brief exposition of the contemporary evolution of the international law of peacebuilding as well as its content. The debates around terminology, as well as when and how this law of peacebuilding should be applied are also alluded to. This discussion, in itself, serves to provide an introductory reflection on the

DOI: 10.4324/9781003462248-1

importance of involving conflict resolution/peace scholars and practitioners in these debates.

Stating the Problem

This book also explores the intersection between international law and peacebuilding, with particular reference to the relationship between lawyers and peace practitioners in this context. The intersection is labelled as the international law of peacebuilding, an aspect of international law with deep historical roots, but which only recently has been conceived as a possibly distinct branch of international law. The work of Carsten Stahn, Jennifer Easterday and Jens Iverson in this respect is particularly notable. Of particular note are their efforts to examine both the historical roots and the current definition(s) as well as the scope of application of the international law of post-conflict peacebuilding.

One may suggest that unlike other branches of international law which have grown in a relatively organic manner, the international law of peacebuilding draws norms from related branches of international law such as the international law on the use of force, international humanitarian law (IHL), international human rights law and international criminal law.

In this sense, it is useful to think of the international law of peacebuilding as a compendium of norms borrowed from allied branches of international law with the specific purpose of assisting the transition from the end of violent conflict (what in peace studies is referred to as negative peace) to a just and sustainable peace (what in peace studies is termed as positive peace).[1] It is in this context that the international law of peacebuilding is intended to operate, as a set of rules derived from various branches of international law that are conducive to the creation of a just and durable peace between hitherto conflicting parties.

The central argument of this book is that this international law of peacebuilding as the law intended to facilitate the transition from negative peace to positive peace needs to be appropriated not just by lawyers but also by those practitioners most deeply and intimately involved with that transition. Conflict resolution practitioners as well as peacebuilding practitioners are evidently a key constituency in this regard. Conflict resolution practitioners are deeply involved in designing processes, mechanisms and actions which assist conflict parties to terminate the use of violence and embark on the processes that will lead to positive peace. Peacebuilding practitioners are intimately involved in assisting in the delivery of actions and the implementation of processes that build positive peace. Therefore, it is apposite that they should be involved in the shaping of this branch of international law far more than they have been hitherto.

Thus, this book will explore a number of interrelated themes. Firstly, what constitutes the international law of peacebuilding and how it has evolved so far are examined. Secondly, the extent to which the development of this branch of law has been largely confined to legal practitioners will be highlighted. Thirdly, the reasons for the limited engagement by peace practitioners will be explored. In this context, an important element is the broader disconnection between legal scholars and practitioners and peace scholars and practitioners. Fourthly, the question of what methods and contexts would be conducive to a greater engagement by conflict and peace practitioners with the international law of peacebuilding will be posed and tentatively answered.

International Law and Armed Conflict

Before considering these themes, it is relevant to place the international law of peacebuilding in the broader framework of international law and armed conflict. While sustained attention to the international law of peacebuilding is relatively new, international law has long contended with issues of war. Evidence of this is found throughout the history of international law. The three individuals most frequently cited as the fathers of international law as an academic discipline are Francisco de Vitoria, Alberico Gentili and Hugo Grotius. It is telling that all three of them wrote books that discussed the laws of war. De Vitoria, who was a theologian and philosopher more than a lawyer, was an exponent of the theory of just war and wrote on this theme in his 1532 work *De Jure belli Hispanorum in barbaros*. Gentili published *De Jure Belli Libri Tres* in 1598, while in 1625, Grotius published his seminal *De Jure Belli Ac Pacis*. Thus, it is evident that in a scholarly sense, international law has been concerned with war from its very inception as an academic discipline. Moreover, it is equally evident the practice of international law has been connected with issues of war and peace from the earliest times.

In practice, the regulation of armed conflict in international law is one of its most ancient branches. A peace treaty known as the Peace Treaty of Kadesh between the Egyptian and Hittite kingdoms dating to 1269 BCE is amongst the earliest known treaties.[2] Peace treaties have remained a constant feature of international law. Rules on when resorting to war is justified were an early interest of the fathers of international law as an academic discipline. Traditionally, these rules of international law concerning war were divided into two distinct branches: *jus ad bellum* and *jus in bello*. The Latin epithets in themselves convey a sense of their antiquity. *Jus ad bellum* is the law on the resort to war, i.e., when is it legitimate to use armed force against another state. This branch of international law is now largely encapsulated in the Charter of the United Nations, particularly in Chapter 7 of the same Charter. *Jus in bello* is the law which regulates the conduct of armed conflict or more precisely the means and methods of warfare. This branch of law is now known as IHL and has been progressively codified and developed since 1864, with the first-ever Geneva Convention for the Amelioration of the Condition of the Wounded in Armies in the Field.

While the resort to war and the conduct of war have been the subject of codification in international law for a considerable amount of time, the aftermath of war has historically not received similar attention. *Jus post bellum* while possessing deep historical roots in theology and philosophy[3] (particularly the development of the concept of just peace) did not become codified in the same manner and to the same extent as *jus ad bellum* and *jus in bello*. The reasons for this lack of development may be manifold.

In the first instance, until the development of conflict and peace studies in the 1960s, the focus in relation to armed conflict was primarily that of ensuring an end to the violent conflict. The end of the armed conflict was the main objective with little attention towards resolving the deep-rooted causes of the conflict. Once that first objective was achieved through a ceasefire or a peace treaty, attention often shifted elsewhere. Secondly, armed conflict often ended with a victorious side imposing a peace treaty on the losing side. The Treaty of Versailles of 1920 is an obvious example of this. The Second World War was also ended on the basis of an unconditional surrender to the victorious powers. Considerations on how to ensure a just and sustainable peace were either of secondary importance or ignored completely. Woodrow Wilson's 14 points, which were an attempt at ensuring sustainable peace, including references to self-determination and international cooperation, could have formed the basis for a *jus post bellum*. However, the peace of Versailles with its punitive provisions was far removed from the Wilsonian idea. Some historians, such as AJP Taylor, even argue that the Versailles Treaty was a significant contributory factor that led to the Second World War.[4]

The Second World War ended with an occupation of Germany by the victorious powers and the ensuing division of Germany into two separate states, which were only reunited in 1990. In the case of Japan, the war also ended with an unconditional surrender and effectively the imposition of a new constitution and political system on Japan. In the case of Germany and France, which had a long tradition of enmity and had experienced three wars within 70 years, the issue of achieving a sustainable peace came about as a result of the efforts of French and German politicians. They jointly decided that they needed to avoid a repetition of the mistakes of the Versailles Treaty and sought close cooperation and enduring friendship through the establishment of the European Coal and Steel Community which would in time become the European Union.[5]

The establishment of the United Nations, while codifying the *jus ad bellum*, did not materially contribute to the evolution of an international law of peacebuilding in its early years. The UN's first decade was taken up with dealing with Cold War concerns, the Israeli-Arab conflict and then the Korean conflict. In these contexts, the UN focused on containment efforts with respect to the Cold War and conflict resolution with respect to the Israeli-Arab and Korean conflicts. In neither of these latter conflicts was there a successful resolution beyond cease-fires which in various forms have lasted ever since.

While the UN was entrusted with the role of maintaining international peace and security, its primary focus was peace-making rather than peacebuilding. Its peacebuilding efforts in institutional form were late in coming. Boutros-Ghali's (1992) publication of an Agenda for Peace was a seminal moment in this respect. An Agenda for Peace highlighted the need for a greater focus on post-conflict peacebuilding within the UN. Eventually, it was only in 2005 that the UN established its Peacebuilding Commission, and even then, the Commission has been mostly devoted to creating country-specific strategies rather than developing guidelines of more general application. The formulation of international law norms is not explicitly included in its mandate.[6]

In fact, as late as 2009, it was possible to accurately comment on the international law of peacebuilding in the following terms: "the international law dimension of peacebuilding seems to have attracted only little attention among scholars and practitioners".[7] A decade later scholarly attention has increased with a number of notable contributions towards shaping the international law of peacebuilding. However, the one major contribution to the development to an international law of peacebuilding; a treaty establishing its foundational norms is still lacking. While *jus ad bellum* has the norms found in the UN Charter and *jus in bello* has the 1949 Geneva Conventions, no equivalent exists which provides clear contours of *jus post bellum*.

Some of the reasons for the absence of a fully fledged international law of peacebuilding have been alluded to. Perhaps one of the most fundamental reasons for this absence is that rules relating to *jus ad bellum* and *jus in bello* are relatively narrow in their application and sphere of action. IHL seeks to regulate the means and methods of warfare during an armed conflict. The whole edifice of IHL may be reduced to five key principles: (i) the distinction between civilians and combatants, (ii) the prohibition of attacking persons who are not involved in the hostilities, (iii) the prohibition of inflicting unnecessary suffering, (iv) the principle of necessity and (v) the principle of proportionality.[8] The UN Charter's provisions on the use of force are narrower still and can be reduced to the prohibition on the use of force except in self-defence or when explicitly authorised by the UN Security Council.[9]

The international law of peacebuilding intended to facilitate the move from a simple cessation of hostilities to a just and sustainable peace is a far more complex undertaking. The international law of peacebuilding needs to assist in securing structural and cultural changes, which are difficult to achieve. The root-causes of each individual armed conflict will be different and the path towards a deep-rooted resolution of the conflict will also likely differ in most cases. Attitudes to how best to deal with atrocities committed during the armed conflict may also differ depending on numerous factors. These may include the severity of such atrocities, on whether they were committed by all sides or primarily by one side and on the cultural attitudes to issues of crime and punishment in the specific context. Most scholars who have considered the matter of the international law of peacebuilding view international human rights norms as an important and integral element of such a law. However, attitudes to human rights generally and international human rights law, in particular, may vary wildly both within the parties to a conflict and more generally across geopolitical contexts.[10]

It is clear that ideas on what peace is and how peace is best achieved and maintained are as old as recorded history. However, it is equally evident that a systematic approach to the understanding of peace and its sustainability owes much to Johan Galtung's efforts in the 1960s. Interest in conflict resolution and peace studies increased expeditiously after the 1960s accompanied not only by non-governmental movements such as the Peace Movement but also by a gradual proliferation of university departments focusing on conflict resolution and peace studies.

During the Cold War, interest also grew in confidence-building measures (CBMs) as a way of resolving frozen conflicts or deep cleavages like the Cold War itself. These CBMs owed a lot to conflict resolution thinking and practice. Indeed, in this context, the international community started adopting such measures which were inspired by conflict resolution methodologies rather than traditional diplomatic and legalistic approaches. Over time, conflict resolution and peace scholars and practitioners have increased our understanding of the nature of peace and peacebuilding and have developed different tools that have assisted in reaching agreements amongst conflicting parties in a variety of settings. The efforts of the conflict resolution and peace scholars and practitioners have had a profound effect on our collective understanding of the complexity of conflict resolution and peacebuilding. The extent to which their professional expertise has influenced and shaped the international law of peacebuilding has certainly not been commensurate.

This book intends to explore some of the reasons why this has been the case and also examine some of the pathways that may be followed to increase the influence of conflict resolution and peace scholars and practitioners on the international law of peacebuilding. In order to do so, it is necessary to have a basic understanding of how international law is created.

The Shaping and Creation of International Law

The creation of international law is mostly associated with big conferences attended by state representatives where those present agree to the adoption of an international treaty. However, the creation of international law in the contemporary world is a more intricate matter. The brief answer is that international law is created by states through two mechanisms: (i) state practices that gradually become widespread and crystallise into unwritten norms of international law (referred to as customary international law) and (ii) contract type agreements between states which are referred to as treaties or conventions.

The concept of customary international law is an important one given that (contrary to what may be assumed) this source of law may have a wider application than treaties. The Statute of the International Court of Justice describes customary international law as "international custom, as evidence of a general practice accepted as law".[11] When there is a dispute as to whether certain conduct is required or allowed by international law and no treaty-based rule is in existence or applicable, the Court will assess what has been the behaviour of states in respect of the conduct in question. It will ask the following questions: how have states behaved in the past in these cases? Have they adopted the practice in question in sufficient numbers? Have they adopted the practice in a uniform and consistent manner? Have they adopted the practice out of expediency/courtesy/efficiency or have they adopted it because they considered themselves legally bound to do so? If the practice has been generally adopted by states in a uniform and consistent manner with a sense of legal obligation, then that practice will have crystallised in a norm of customary law which all states have an obligation to comply with.

The abolition of slavery is a good example. The prohibition of slavery is now a matter regulated by treaty law (several treaties prohibit slavery such as the International Covenant on Civil and Political Rights). However, until the early 20th century there was no treaty rule prohibiting slavery. Its prohibition was a matter regulated by customary international law. Gradually from the beginning of the 19th century, states began progressively banning the slave trade and then slavery itself. By the 1880s, a rule of customary law prohibiting the slave trade and slavery was in place. When, under the auspices of the League of Nations, the Convention to Suppress the Slave Trade and Slavery was adopted in 1926, it was simply codifying an existing rule of customary international law.[12]

The reference to customary international law being of wider application than treaty law is a result of the fact that the rules of customary international law, generally, apply to all states. There is no requirement that a state opt-in or formally adhere to these rules (as is required for treaty-based rules). The mere fact of being a state within the international community is sufficient to create an obligation to comply with such customary rules of international law. Customary rules of international law allow states to opt out of them through a process known as the "persistent objector", whereby a state unwilling to be bound by an emerging rule of customary law must consistently and persistently formally object to that practice before it has crystallised into a rule of law. Finally, such a possibility to object does not apply to a very few fundamental rules of international law (such as the prohibition of genocide and of aggression), which are known as *jus cogens*, i.e., rules of international law that may never be derogated from.

However, given that it is being argued that the international law of peacebuilding is primarily lacking a treaty text to serve as its foundational document, the treaties are of more relevance in this context. This narrow answer, however, gives rise to further questions. Which are the forces that drive states to adopt certain practices in a given context or drive them to enter into contractual agreements with other states?

The broad answer to the question of who creates international law is thus a complex one as it tries to identify the forces which drive state actions. Given that states are in the words of the Nuremberg Tribunal "abstract entities", it is difficult to ascertain with a sufficient degree of certainty the attribution of state actions to particular forces. Nevertheless, this is an important question for the purposes of the matters discussed in this book. The answer will assist in exploring the forces that have given rise to the norms that constitute the content of the international law of peacebuilding.

So, while it is evident that international law is created by states, the question of who shapes international law is not amenable to such a direct and simple answer. A case which will assist in elucidating this matter is the creation of IHL. The first ever convention that created norms in this branch of international law is the aforementioned Geneva Convention for the Amelioration of the Condition of the Wounded in Armies in the Field of 22 August 1864. The Convention was initially signed by 12 states including Switzerland, Italy, France, the Netherlands, Spain, Portugal and a number of German states such as Prussia (which in 1870 were absorbed into Germany). Thus, it is clear who created the first codified rules of IHL. One only needs to verify the records to obtain a list of the states that ratified the convention and thus created the law. However, this is only a partial answer to the question. One may argue that the creator of the Geneva Convention in a deeper sense was Henri Dunant or at least the International Committee of the Red Cross which he helped create. The history of Henri Dunant and his experiences at the Battle of Solferino are well-known, as are his subsequent efforts to create the ICRC, which in turn promoted the adoption of the first Geneva Convention. To this day, the ICRC maintains a crucial role in promoting the adoption of new rules of IHL through its advocacy efforts.

Generally, the shaping of international law (particularly international law derived from treaties) is obviously driven by the entities that form the institutions of the state in the executive, legislative and judicial branches. Each state has its own rules that regulate whether and how a state will become a party to a treaty. In some states, the executive has an unfettered right to decide, while in other states the treaty-making power is held by the legislative branch and may be subject to judicial review. Nevertheless, the initial decision to promote the adoption of a treaty on the international stage is the result of a number of factors such as the existence of an international non-governmental campaign for the regulation of a matter of international concern, the occurrence of an event which has special impact on the international community as a whole and the existence of a group of like-minded states pushing a particular agenda.

In this context, the pathways through which the Statute of the International Criminal Court (ICC) was eventually adopted is an instructive case study and merits a relatively detailed examination as it illustrates admirably the various factors that may come into play in the formation of international law. The adoption of the London Agreement of August 1945 (a treaty between the USSR, the United States, the United Kingdom and France) established the International Military Tribunal known as the Nuremberg Tribunal. The Agreement also set up the rudiments of what would become international criminal law (such as stipulating the crimes which would be punishable by the Tribunal). The Agreement came about in a very specific context, i.e., the end of the Second World War and the attendant discoveries of various atrocities, chief of which was the Holocaust.

The Nuremberg Trials in their entirety (i.e. the Agreement as well as the Tribunal's judgment) provided the framework for an embryonic international criminal law by establishing individual criminal responsibility under international law, the crimes under international law, available defences, the rights of the accused, etc. This embryonic framework was soon after endorsed by the UN General Assembly in 1946.[13] In 1948, the General Assembly also adopted the text of the Genocide Convention which *inter alia* created genocide as a distinct crime under international law, thus adding to the evolving structure of international criminal law. The history of the adoption of this treaty is equally instructive with a pivotal role played by an individual, namely, the Polish lawyer Raphael Lemkin who was intransigent and inexhaustible in his campaigning for its adoption.[14]

At this point in time, the international community was also considering the possibility of establishing a permanent ICC as evidenced in Article 6 of the 1948 Genocide Convention.[15] Due to Cold War tensions, the plan to establish a permanent ICC was shelved. However, the idea of establishing such a court was revived in 1989 when the Permanent Representative of Trinidad and Tobago to the President of the UN General Assembly made the suggestion in the context of international drug trafficking.[16] Given that at that time the international political juncture was a positive one (with the ending of the Cold War only a few months away), the idea garnered support and the International Law Commission was tasked with commencing work on a set of draft articles for a treaty. While this work proceeded, two events occurred which had an impact on the pace at which these efforts would eventually materialise into a treaty; one may also argue that without these two events, the ICC may have never been established. In 1992, war broke out in the former Yugoslavia. While the war in Slovenia was very brief and the one in Croatia also relatively brief, the war in Bosnia Herzegovina raged for several years with thousands of civilian casualties and many reports of atrocities. As the war in Bosnia Herzegovina proceeded, Rwanda was the site of one of the worst episodes of genocide in the 20th century with an estimated 800,000 killed within a few months.

These two events led the UN Security Council (which in both instances had failed to exercise effectively its authority in dealing with threats to international peace and security) to take a reactive and legalistic approach by establishing two Ad Hoc Tribunals to prosecute individuals who had committed war crimes, crimes against humanity and genocide in the former Yugoslavia and Rwanda respectively. The two tribunals developed international criminal law significantly through their constitutive charters and their numerous judgments. Their establishment also persuaded many states that a permanent ICC would be a necessity in the contemporary world.

In parallel with the establishment of the tribunals, two groups formed which would play an important role in securing the adoption of the text that would become the Statute of the ICC. The first grouping was composed of 60 states from around the globe, termed the "like-minded group", who drove the negotiating process forward and were instrumental in achieving a truly independent ICC. The second grouping was an alliance of 25 non-governmental organisations set up in 1995 to campaign domestically and internationally for the establishment of a permanent ICC.[17] This alliance which was entitled Coalition for a Permanent ICC owed a lot to the human rights movement which had developed in a number of states and internationally from the 1960s onwards. This strategic alliance between a group of states and a group of NGOs has been credited with the successful adoption of the Rome Statute:

> Creating the International Criminal Court (ICC) at the end of the twentieth century stands as the outstanding achievement in international human rights during that decade. Cooperation between an extraordinary network of NGOs and a group of activist states, most of them small and at the periphery of "high politics," accounted for this success.[18]

The evolution of international criminal law was thus influenced by (i) events such as World War Two, the Rwandan genocide and the Yugoslav war, (ii) a political initiative at a propitious time (Trinidad and Tobago's proposal in 1989), (iii) international non-governmental advocacy and (iv) a group of states pushing the agenda forward. This helps to illustrate the complexities that play into the creation of international law, especially in areas where states are particularly sensitive to issues of sovereignty, such as in issues relating to human rights and criminal jurisdiction. It also shows that there is scope for non-state actors to play a role in shaping international law, which is an issue that lies at the heart of this book.

The Evolution of the International Law of Peacebuilding

There are various scholarly examinations of the deep historical roots of the international law of peacebuilding, which illustrate *inter alia* the relationship between *jus post bellum* and the just war tradition.[19] However, the focus of this book is on how the current normative content of this law is being shaped and by whom. As mentioned earlier, until very recently, there was little attention paid to the international law of peacebuilding in practice or academic contexts. The first sustained efforts at examining the existence of an international law of peacebuilding and what its content, scope of application and extent may be dated from the first decade of the new millennium and have greatly intensified in the past 5–10 years.

The definition of the international law of post-conflict peacebuilding adopted here is essentially the one offered by Jens Iverson as a body of law that should apply in the transition from armed conflict to sustainable peace.[20] It should also be clear that the precise contours of this body of law are still being discussed and debated. The elements which are suggested as forming a fundamental part of the international law of peacebuilding are (i) the international law on annexation (if territories are annexed, how can a sustainable peace be achieved? Crimea is a current example), (ii) the law on self-determination of peoples (What is its exact content? Does international law allow secession? The answers to these and other questions may have an impact on achieving sustainable peace in territories such as Kosovo.), (iii) international human rights law (ensuring respect for fundamental rights and principles such as non-discrimination are critical in transitions from armed conflict to peace), (iv) international criminal law (should perpetrators of the most egregious crimes in international law such as genocide and war crimes be punished and, if so, in what fora?) and (v) the rights and responsibilities that emerge from the doctrine of the Responsibility to Protect (R2P), especially the issue of the Responsibility to Rebuild. Given that the international law of post-conflict peacebuilding is still in the process of formation, this is certainly a non-exhaustive list. However, it helps to illustrate the range and complexity of the issues with which the international law of peacebuilding needs to contend.

In this context, it is important to note that given that the international law of peacebuilding draws from other allied branches of public international law, some of its constituent elements (at least as defined by legal scholars) emerged well before attention to the international law of peacebuilding materialised. One such area of public international law is, in fact, related to *jus ad bellum* and refers to the status of annexation in international law. At least until the end of World War One, annexation was accepted as a method whereby states could acquire territory.[21] The situation only began to change with the adoption of the Covenant of the League of Nations which guaranteed the territorial integrity of states and then with the Kellogg Briand Pact which outlawed war as a means of achieving political aims. As discussed above, the adoption of the UN Charter in 1945 codified the prohibition of the use of force and simultaneously guaranteed the independence, sovereignty and territorial integrity of states. As a result, the acquisition of territory through use of force (i.e. annexation) became clearly and conclusively illegal under international law. The protection of the territorial integrity of states from being infringed as a result of the use of force was evident in the case of Cyprus, where in Resolution 541 of 1983 the Security Council called on all states to refrain from recognising the Turkish Republic of Northern Cyprus. Most legal scholars maintain that the prohibition of annexation forms part of the emerging international law of peacebuilding.

However, the rule against any infringement on the territorial integrity has since the 1990s been under attack from another rule of public international law, i.e., the right of self-determination of peoples. This concept of self-determination emerged in the context of the First World War, but became more firmly established and acquired normative status in the context of the UN Charter and more specifically the decolonisation process of the 1960s. However, by the 1970s, the number of people living under clearly colonial rule had diminished to insignificance. At the same time, a more difficult and potentially destabilising question arose which went beyond the applicability of the right to self-determination to colonial territories. The question referred to the right to self-determination of groups linked by ethnicity, language or religion (or a combination of these factors) who lived within states which were not of a clearly colonial nature. This mainly referred to "minorities" or indigenous populations which inhabited existing states where borders had been arbitrarily drawn (usually by colonial powers or by victorious powers in post-war scenarios or as compromises to avoid wars).

These situations where minorities or indigenous populations exist within established states (as for example the Basque minority within Spain or Russians in Estonia) raise the question as to whether the right to self-determination is applicable to them or whether it is applicable but to a lesser extent; or not applicable at all. According to Cassese, self-determination is only clearly established as a matter of international law as "anti-colonial standard, as a ban on foreign occupation, and as a requirement that all racial groups be given full access to government".[22] Thus, beyond the clear confines of colonial rule, foreign occupation and apartheid there is no legal certainty as to whether self-determination is applicable, and if it is in what way it should be applied.

This general consensus seems to be that secession in the context of the exercise of the right to self-determination is not an option normally available outside colonial contexts. However, there seems to be a caveat that territorial integrity may be jeopardised by a state not complying with the duty of protecting minorities from oppression. The threshold of non-compliance required to trigger off a right to secession seems to be rather high. The Canadian Supreme Court in the Quebec Secession Case highlights the notion that the right to secede to exercise self-determination only arose in "the most extreme cases and, even then, under carefully defined circumstances" having regard to the parallel need for respect for the territorial integrity of states. Crawford argues that "international law allows (in extreme cases of oppression) remedial secession to discrete people within a state".[23] The situation arising in Kosovo seems to validate Crawford's view. Although the International Court of Justice's Advisory Opinion on the legality of Kosovo's unilateral declaration of independence did not enter the merits of this issue, the emergence of Kosovo as a state recognised by numerous other states seems to suggest that "remedial secession" may be successful in law and practice. The Court, in the Kosovo, case did however indicate that this matter was susceptible to disagreement and one may not give a conclusive answer to the question of whether "remedial secession" is a right under international law. The Court in fact stated that:

> Whether outside the context of non-self-governing territories and peoples subject to alien subjugation, domination and exploitation, the international law of self-determination confers upon part of the population of an existing State, a right to separate is, however, a subject on which radically different views were expressed…Similar differences existed regarding whether international law provides for a right of "remedial secession", and, if so, in what circumstances.[24]

The emphasis on the strong differences expressed with respect to the applicability of the right to self-determination in non-colonial situations lead one to suggest that whereas it is impossible to state that a right of "remedial secession" exists, "remedial secession" may in certain circumstances be successful and allowed by international law. One may also add that the success or otherwise of such "remedial secession" will be determined by *de facto* political considerations and criteria of effectiveness rather than by strictly legal ones.

The Kosovo situation thus brings to the fore the aspect of public international law which impacts on the international law of peacebuilding, namely, the law on the self-determination of peoples. The international law of peacebuilding will be hampered considerably if the legal content of this right remains unclear. The annexation of Crimea in 2014 by the Russian Federation, together with the annexation of eastern parts of the Ukraine following the invasion of February 2022 are a stark reminder of the dangers associated with this unregulated right of self-determination in undermining the principle of territorial integrity and the principle that states may not use force to acquire territory.

One of the major factors drawing attention to the desirability of an international legal framework intended to sustain and support a durable peace centred around the relationship between international human rights norms and peace processes. The argument that human rights norms and institutions were an important part of post-conflict societies was evident from the South African and Northern Irish experiences. In both of these contexts human rights were viewed as indispensable pillars of the post-conflict societies given that in both conflicts discriminatory practices were a critical part of the conflict itself (in the case of South Africa racial discrimination was the essential content of the conflict).

Thus, the inclusion of human rights components in peace agreements based on international human rights norms became a standard practice encouraged by UN resolutions and subject to significant scholarly attention.[25] Indeed, it has been argued that international human rights law has become part of the *lex pacificatoria* (the law of peace treaties). The reasons for the central importance attributed to international human rights norms in creating the post-conflict structures included the proliferation of international human rights treaties and the UN emphasis on human rights across its activities together with a recognition that human rights norms, institutions and processes may contribute to de-escalate sentiments of discrimination, unfairness and injustice.[26]

As highlighted earlier, another branch of public international law which grew exponentially in the 1990s was international criminal law. This branch of international law has also impacted on the growth in interest and attention towards the international law of peacebuilding. In fact, one of the mantras used by the NGO community in advocating for a permanent international criminal law was "no peace without justice". The argument used by these NGOs and by the like-minded group of states was that without justice for those who had suffered atrocities such as crimes against humanity and genocide, there could be no sustainable peace. As shall be discussed in Chapter 4, this theorem that there can be no peace without justice, while attracting considerable support was not universally endorsed and in particular some conflict resolution and peacebuilding scholars and practitioners considered it to be an obstacle to making peace rather than part of the solution.[27]

Nevertheless, the concept that persons accused of the most serious crimes under international law should not go unpunished took root in international law. This "fight against impunity" was also adopted by the UN which endorsed it in various fora.[28] The adoption of this stance was already having some practical consequences in 1999 when the UN Secretary General's representative to the Sierra Leone peace negotiations added a handwritten disclaimer to his signature stating the UN did not recognise any amnesties for gross human rights violations.[29] Since then, the UN has officially always condemned impunity for mass atrocities including crimes under international law. The extent to which this norm represents a rule of customary international law is disputable. However, most scholars writing on the international law of peacebuilding view the matter of impunity as an integral part of the legal infrastructure in post-conflict contexts.

In the 1990s, the international community also witnessed the evolution of the doctrine known as the R2P, which partially influenced the content of the international law of peacebuilding. The doctrine arose in the context of the Balkan Wars and the NATO intervention in Kosovo. In the first case, the international community was criticised (particularly the UN) for having failed to protect civilians from gross human rights violations such as genocide and crimes against humanity. In the second case, NATO acted militarily (and in breach of the UN Charter) to stop the repression against the Kosovar population on the basis that if the UN was unable to act, there still remained a humanitarian imperative to protect civilians. In 1999, then UN Secretary General, Kofi Annan highlighted the need to bridge the gap between these two situations and repeated this call in his 2000 Millennium Report: "if humanitarian intervention is, indeed, an unacceptable assault on sovereignty, how should we respond to a Rwanda, to a Srebrenica, to gross and systematic violation of human rights that offend every precept of our common humanity?"[30]

The question was the subject of much debate in the first years of the new millennium[31] and eventually at the 2005 World Summit the R2P was adopted as a principle by the UN and its Member States through a Resolution of the General Assembly. This doctrine is still the subject of controversy as some fear it may be used to legitimise the use of armed force in contravention of the UN Charter (i.e. the current jus ad bellum). While in the heyday of 2005, there was much official talk and academic discussion of the doctrine, this attention has waned considerably. Of particular interest in the context of peacebuilding is that in parallel with the R2P arose the Responsibility to Rebuild after military interventions undertaken in the R2P context. While references to the doctrine abound in UN Security Council Resolutions, the high waterline of the R2P doctrine in practice was arguably the UN Security Council mandated intervention in Libya adopted on the basis of the R2P.[32]

While following the perceived failures in Libya and its non-application in Syria and Yemen amongst others R2P has lost its early shine, it may be argued that in the case of Libya, the failure was not so much in the R2P but rather in implementing the responsibility to rebuild after the military intervention. Indeed, in the context of the international law of peacebuilding the focus on the responsibility to rebuild as part of the law has been sustained. Scholars who have discussed the evolution of the international law of peacebuilding have sought to integrate the responsibility to rebuild into the international law of peacebuilding.[33]

What does the responsibility to rebuild actually entail? As originally envisaged, the responsibility to rebuild referred to the obligation on the international community to provide assistance with recovery, reconstruction and reconciliation. The exact contours of this responsibility will depend on the context of the conflict. In a context such as Kosovo or Libya, where there were external actors involved in the use of force, the responsibility of these actors should be more acute. In other contexts, such as civil wars where no external actors are involved in the use of force, the responsibility will primarily rest on the state emerging out of conflict with the international community as a whole having a responsibility to assist as requested. One notes that the content of the responsibility to rebuild may be extremely wide and debatable.

Assistance with recovery may mean several things contemporaneously: the rebuilding of the civil service, the fiscal system, the judiciary, the police force, health systems, public broadcasting, security forces and other state agencies can all form part of the recovery process. Is the state emerging out of conflict at liberty to decide the nature of these rebuilding efforts, with the responsibility of the international community limited to providing funding and technical assistance? Or should there be international law norms which constrain the choices made by the state/s involved? Such constraints may be based on notions of rule of law, popular legitimacy, compatibility with international human rights standards, etc.

The recovery process may also include the reintegration into civilian life of ex-combatants. This is a subject area which has also seen increased attention and interest amongst the peacebuilding community at governmental and non-governmental levels as well as amongst scholars.[34] As yet, there are no codified international law norms which govern this matter, although the UN has since 2006 adopted a set of standards on disarmament, demobilisation and reintegration of ex-combatants.[35] An exception to the lack of codified norms in this field is the reintegration of child soldiers, which is considered separately given that international law clearly prohibits the recruitment of child soldiers. The Optional Protocol to the Convention on the Rights of the Child on the involvement of children in armed conflict which was adopted in the year 2000 specifically requires governments to take measures to demobilise and rehabilitate former child soldiers and to reintegrate them into society.

Assistance with reconstruction is relatively a more straightforward concept with an emphasis on infrastructural rebuilding. In this case, the rebuilding of the physical infrastructure of the state/s includes power generation, hospitals, schools, housing, etc. While this may seem relatively uncontroversial, there may also be questions of where such infrastructures are built or not built, which should take precedence and how was the funding of these, usually, large projects managed. Should the international law of peacebuilding regulate issues like corruption, profiteering, popular participation in decision-making, location, etc.? And who should the responsibility to fund this reconstruction fall upon exactly? Finally, assistance with reconciliation is perhaps the most problematic aspect. What kind of reconciliation should be undertaken? Who should decide on reconciliation measures? Does reconciliation include legal mechanisms referred to above in the context of international criminal law? In this context of reconciliation, what are the respective responsibilities of the state/s emerging out of conflict and the international community and what is reconciliation for groups who have never had good relations?

These are just some of the questions which the international law of peacebuilding is required to answer. It is submitted that for the international law of peacebuilding to take its place alongside *jus ad bellum* and *jus in bello* as a well-established part of international law, these questions require answering in as clear a manner as possible. This will require two parallel processes. On the one hand, those aspects of international law which remain unclear need to be settled (such as the exact content and consequences of the right to self-determination and clearer rules on the obligations associated with the responsibility to rebuild).

On the other hand, the international law of peacebuilding requires a foundational legal text which clarifies which rules of international law it should encompass and when it should apply. The latter issue for example has drawn different responses. Some scholars argue it should be applied on a temporal basis (i.e. from the end of the violent conflict through a peace treaty), while others argue that elements of the international law of peacebuilding should be applied even before the armed conflict is formally terminated. Another related matter is the application of the international law of peacebuilding to frozen conflicts where a ceasefire has been achieved but the conflict has not been formally terminated (such as the Cypriot conflict). Should the international law of peacebuilding apply in these contexts? In Cyprus, at least, different views exist on this matter.[36]

Some questions also exist as to whether the international law of post-conflict peacebuilding is equivalent to the concept of transitional justice, which has attracted significant attention since at least the 1990s. While different views exist on this matter, for the purposes of this book, transitional justice is considered a distinct and different concept from the law of peacebuilding. The differences may be summarised as follows. Transitional justice is of broader application because it applies not only to transitions from periods of international or domestic armed conflict to periods of peace but also to political transitions, such as the post-Cold War transitions in Eastern Europe in the 1990s. These transitions include elements of structural violence (human rights violations such as the lack of freedom of expression or political participation) and may include physical violence (such as torture) but are not characterised as armed conflict in the accepted sense of both international law and peace studies. In this sense, transitional justice covers more situations and contexts than the international law of peacebuilding which as forming part of the international law concerning armed conflict (the *jus ad bellum*, *jus in bello* and *jus post bellum* triad) is limited in scope to such situations of armed conflict.

The second fundamental distinction is that transitional justice only focuses on responses to systematic or large-scale human rights abuses. The aim of transitional justice is to provide "redress to victims and creates or enhances opportunities for the transformation of the political systems, conflicts, and other conditions that may have been at the root of the abuses".[37] As illustrated above scholars consider that the international law of peacebuilding includes within its purview some of the same concerns, particularly drawing on norms of international criminal law. However, the scope of the international law of peacebuilding is wider than just redress for human rights violations. Issues like the law of self-determination, annexation, responsibility to rebuild, and the reintegration of members of armed forces are not an integral part of transitional justice, while they are considered to be part of the international law of peacebuilding. While this outline of the evolution of elements of the international law of peacebuilding is not exhaustive, it suffices to highlight some of the norms which may constitute the international law of peacebuilding and also some of the gaps that need to be addressed.

Conclusion

This chapter has argued that the international law of peacebuilding is a branch of law in the process of being born (to use a phrase from the international law of statehood[38]). It is not a fully formed nor firmly established branch of international law. However, it is a necessary part of international law. It is in the interests of the international community not only to end the armed conflict but also to ensure that it does not return. The maintenance of international peace and security, which is the key objective of the UN, requires not only regulation of the circumstances when armed force may be lawfully used but also norms that assist in avoiding the resort or return to armed conflict.

The fact that the international law of peacebuilding is still "in formation" provides opportunities which are less available in the context of long-standing norms of international law. In particular, it is still possible for diverse actors to shape its content and scope of application. As highlighted in this chapter, the shaping and creation of international law is amenable to numerous factors and actors. As shall become evident in the subsequent chapter, efforts to shape and create the law of peacebuilding have, so far, been almost exclusively led by legal scholars and practitioners.

It is the central argument of this book that the content of the international law of peacebuilding will be improved if practitioners and scholars from the conflict resolution and peacebuilding communities are engaged in shaping it, more than has hitherto been the case. Conflict resolution and peacebuilding practitioners have a key stake in this endeavour as actors who are regularly involved in designing and facilitating conflict resolution efforts, ceasefires and peace agreements.

Peacebuilding practitioners remain on the ground once a ceasefire or peace agreement has been agreed to, in order to assist in the processes of maintaining and building peace. The community of peacebuilding practitioners often includes both international actors, national institutions and local civil society organisations. Thus, they bring a width and breadth of experiences and skills that lawyers and international law may greatly benefit from in creating an international law of peacebuilding that meets the requirements of peace and is practicable to implement on the ground. Having norms of international law which are routinely flouted or marginalised is counterproductive for the whole edifice of international law. The involvement of practitioners who play a critical role in the implementation of the international law of peacebuilding may add to the likelihood that the law of peacebuilding will be more regularly and widely observed.

Notes

1 The distinction between "negative peace", understood as the absence of physical violence, and "positive peace", understood as the existence of harmonious relationships between the previously conflicting parties, was first highlighted by Johan

Galtung. In his first exposition of positive peace in 1964, Galtung referred to human integration as being the cornerstone of positive peace. He later developed the concept of positive peace as the absence of structural violence (as well as physical violence).

2 See United Nations. (2023). Replica of Peace Treaty between Hattusilis and Ramses II. https://www.un.org/ungifts/replica-peace-treaty-between-hattusilis-and-ramses-ii#:~:text=This%20Kadesh%20Peace%20Treaty%20is,Ramses%2C%20Pharaoh%20of%20the%20Egyptians (accessed February 13, 2023).

3 For a detailed discussion of the relationship between the Jus Post Bellum and just war theory see Iverson, J. (2021). *Jus Post Bellum: The Rediscovery, Foundations, and Future of the Law of Transforming War into Peace*. Leiden: Brill Nijhoff.

4 Taylor, A. J. P. (1961). *The Origins of the Second World War*. London: Hamish Hamilton.

5 The Schuman Declaration of May 1950 referred specifically to world peace and the age-old enmity between France and Germany as well as to the creation of a cooperative framework which "will make it plain that any war between France and Germany becomes not merely unthinkable, but materially impossible".

6 The Peacebuilding Commission has four aspects to its mandate: (a) to bring sustained international attention to sustaining peace and to provide political accompaniment and advocacy to countries affected by conflict, with their consent, (b) to promote an integrated, strategic and coherent approach to peacebuilding, (c) to serve a bridging role amongst the principal organs and relevant entities of the United Nations and (d) to serve as a platform to convene all relevant actors within and outside the United Nations, to develop and share good practices in peacebuilding, including on institution-building, and to ensure predictable financing to peacebuilding.

7 Schaller, C. (2009). Towards an International Legal Framework for Post-Conflict Peacebuilding, SWP Research Paper, RP 3 (February): 5. https://www.swp-berlin.org/publications/products/research_papers/2009_RP03_slr_ks.pdf.

8 International Committee of the Red Cross. (2011). How Does Law Protect in War? Fundamental Principles of IHL. https://casebook.icrc.org/law/fundamentals-ihl (accessed February 13, 2023).

9 The international law on the use of force may be identified in *Charter of the United Nations*, 26 June 1945, Art. 2(4), 42 and 51 (entered into force 24 October 1945).

10 For example, within the Northern Irish conflict there are divergent views on human rights between the two main communities. See Grech, O. (2017). *Human Rights and the Northern Ireland Conflict*. New York: Routledge.

11 *Statute of the International Court of Justice*, United Nations, 26 June 1945, Article 38 (1) (b) (entered into force 24 October 24, 1945).

12 The Brussels Conference Act of 1890 prohibited slavery but this was a more limited prohibition and the Act was limited to a few states and lacked detailed rules.

13 Affirmation of the Principles of International Law recognised by the *Charter of the Nuremberg Tribunal*. United Nations General Assembly, 1 October 1946, Resolution 95 (I) of the United Nations General Assembly (entered into force 11 December 1946).

14 For a detailed examination of Lemkin's role see Irvin-Erickson, D. (2016). *Raphaël Lemkin and the Concept of Genocide*. Philadelphia, PA: University of Pennsylvania Press.

15 The article states: Persons charged with genocide or any of the other acts enumerated in article III shall be tried by a competent tribunal of the State in the territory of which the act was committed, **or by such international penal tribunal as may have jurisdiction** with respect to those Contracting Parties which shall have accepted its jurisdiction.

16 United Nations. (2004). Letter Dated 15 September 1989 from the Permanent Representative of Trinidad and Tobago to the United Nations President of the General Assembly. https://digitallibrary.un.org/record/73974?ln=zh_CN (accessed on February 13, 2023).

17 Coalition for the International Criminal Court. Our Story, the Coalition for the International Criminal Court. https://www.coalitionfortheicc.org/node/1072 (accessed on February 13, 2023).

18 Welch Jr, C. E. and Watkins, A. F. (2011). Extending Enforcement: The Coalition for the International Criminal Court. *Human Rights Quarterly* 30: 928.

19 Stahn, C. and Iverson, J. (2020). *Just Peace after Conflict: Jus Post Bellum and the Justice of* Peace. Oxford: Oxford University Press: 29–47.

20 Stahn and Iverson. *Just Peace after Conflict*: 65–78.

21 The annexation of Alsace-Lorraine following the Franco-Prussian War of 1870 and of Bosnia Herzegovina by the Austro-Hungarian Empire in 1908 are two examples.

22 Cassese, A. (2005). *International Law*, Oxford: University Press. 60.

23 Crawford, J. , (2007). *The Creation of States in International Law*, Oxford: Oxford University Press. 114.

24 Accordance with international law of the unilateral declaration of independence in respect of Kosovo, International Court of Justice, 22nd July 2010.

25 See, for example, Bell, C. (2003). *Human Rights and Peace Agreement*. Oxford: Oxford University Press.

26 Grech, *Human Rights and the Northern Ireland Conflict.*

27 A particularly strong rejection of the centrality of human rights in conflict resolution is found in an Anonymous article Anon. (1996). Human Rights in Peace Negotiations. *Human Rights Quarterly* 18 (2): 249–258.

28 See, for example, Vienna Declaration and Programme of Action, 25 June 1993, Part II Para 91 (entered into force 25 June 1993) as well as the United Nations Set of principles for the protection and promotion of human rights through action to combat impunity, 1997, E/CN.4/Sub.2/1997/20/Rev.1 (updated in 2005).

29 The UN Secretary General's Special Representative to the Sierra Leone Peace Negotiations had added a disclaimer to the peace agreement signed on 7 July 1999 in Lomé, Togo, which provided a general amnesty for all acts committed during the pursuit of the internal armed conflict since 1991. The Special Representative added the disclaimer that the UN does not recognise the amnesty as applying to international crimes of genocide, crimes against humanity, war crimes and other serious violations of international humanitarian law.

30 Annan, K. (2000). *We the Peoples: The Role of the United Nations in the 21st Century*. New York: United Nations.

31 In particular, the doctrine was shaped by the International Commission on Intervention and State Sovereignty which issued a report entitled The Responsibility to Protect in 2001. This was followed in 2004 by the report of the UN's High-Level Panel on Threats, Challenges and Change entitled "A more secure world: our shared responsibility" and then in 2005 the Secretary-General issued the report "In Larger Freedom: towards development, security and human rights for all".

32 In UN SC Resolution 1970 of 2011, the responsibility of Libya to protect its civilians was expressly mentioned and reiterated in UN SC Resolution 1973 of 2011 where the use of all necessary measures was authorised to protect the Libyan civilian population.

33 See, for example, Hilpold, P. (2015). Jus Post Bellum and the Responsibility to Rebuild – Identifying the Contours of an Ever More Important Aspect of R2P. *Journal of International Humanitarian Legal Studies* 6: 284–305.

34 The literature on the reintegration of ex-combatants is vast. See, for example, Berdal, M. and Ucko, D. H. (2013). Introduction to the DDR Forum: Rethinking

the Reintegration of Former Combatants. *International Peacekeeping* 20 (3): 316–320; Rolston, B. (2007). Demobilization and Reintegration of Ex-Combatants: The Irish Case in International Perspective. *Social and Legal Studies* 16 (2): 259–280; Kaplan, O. and Nussio, E. (2018). Community Counts: The Social Reintegration of Ex-combatants in Colombia. *Conflict Management and Peace Science* 35 (2): 132–153.

35 United Nations DDR Integrated Disarmament, Demobilization and Reintegration Standards (IDDRS). (2006) (last updated 2019) https://www.unddr.org/operational-guide-iddrs/ (accessed February 13, 2023).

36 Interviews conducted by the author in Cyprus with lawyers revealed they were sceptical about its application given one could not build peace until the illegality of the invasion was resolved. Conversely, scholars from the political science and international relations fields thought that peacebuilding initiatives had long been undertaken in Cyprus so there was no reason for an international law of peacebuilding not to be applied.

37 United Nations. (2008). What is transitional justice? A backgrounder, available at https://www.un.org/peacebuilding/sites/www.un.org.peacebuilding/files/documents/26_02_2008_background_note.pdf (accessed on February 23, 2023)

38 In the law of statehood, a state which is still in formation is also referred to as *in statu nascendi*.

2 The International Law of Post-Conflict Peacebuilding

Concepts and Directions

Introduction

This chapter will provide a summary of the main academic literature on the international law of peacebuilding. The purpose of this chapter will be two-fold. Initially, it will summarise the main arguments that have been developed around the concept of the international law of peacebuilding.

It will then provide an analysis of the academic/professional disciplines of the authors of the key literature and the way in which their disciplinary frameworks determine how they approach the topic. The literature examined will centre the key ideas around "international law of peacebuilding" and *jus post bellum* on both of which have been introduced in the preceding chapter.

In exploring the literature on the international law of peacebuilding, the areas where frictions between lawyers and conflict resolvers are evident will be highlighted. These areas include the recognition of *de facto* situations brought about by the use of force, international criminal law and post-conflict human rights guarantees. The chapter will conclude by asking whether (apart from lawyers and legal philosophers) conflict resolution and peace (CRP) scholars and practitioners should also be key stakeholders in the quest to formulate and progressively develop the international law of peacebuilding.

Before focusing on any of the above matters, it is apposite to include a note on terminology. Throughout this whole exploration, I use the term "peacebuilding" by which I mean the processes through which communities within states and states amongst themselves progress from a condition of negative peace to a condition approximating (as much as possible) positive peace. However, it must be acknowledged that the term "peacebuilding" has become a contested one in the CRP community as is the term "post-conflict". In terms of peacebuilding, Vivienne Jabri has critiqued the term as a potential avenue for postcolonial empire-building.[1] While Richard Rubenstein and Michael English have referred to its "generality, vagueness, and normative nature" which, "sometimes obscure answers to essential questions about the sources and methods of combatting structural violence".[2]

DOI: 10.4324/9781003462248-2

Without prejudice to the validity of these and other criticisms, the term international law of peacebuilding has – as shall become more apparent in this chapter – become the accepted term in the budding field. Apart from pragmatic considerations, I would also suggest that confined to the admittedly limited definition provided above, it encapsulates what this branch of law should contribute towards (the approximation of positive peace). The term "post-conflict" is equally contested as peacebuilding activity (understood as an activity which moves the actors and structures in a conflict setting towards positive peace) may be undertaken even during the persistence of violent conflict. This is evidently true. However, it is equally evident that the focus during the period of violent conflict is the attaining of negative peace as a first step. Once this first step is achieved, then the focus must shift to peacebuilding for positive peace. This is the definition of post-conflict I adopt throughout this study. The period during which sustained direct violence is absent, whether or not there is a formal peace agreement. In the case of Cyprus, the sustained ceasefire that has prevailed for several decades would in my view qualify for the application of the post-conflict epithet. This matter is discussed further below with respect to the scope of application of the law of post-conflict peacebuilding. Having considered these terminological difficulties, the focus returns to the international law of peacebuilding.

As highlighted in the previous chapter, the international law of peacebuilding started being conceived as a potentially distinct area of international law in the past 20 years. The main framers of the debate are mostly associated with Dutch universities, which is hardly surprising given their historic association with international law from the time of Grotius. The seeds of the contemporary interest in the international law of peacebuilding may be found at the end of the Cold War when the UN under the guidance of Secretary-General Boutros Boutros-Ghali started developing the concept of peacebuilding as part of its core mandate.

In this context, the publication of An Agenda for Peace in 1992 was a seminal moment.[3] This report sought to clarify a number of concepts that the UN began to engage with in a structured way including preventive diplomacy, peace-making, peace-keeping and post-conflict peacebuilding. The report was framed as a response by the Secretary-General to a request by the Security-Council (meeting, unusually, at the level of Heads of States in January 1992) for recommendations on how to make the UN more efficient and responsive in terms of preventive diplomacy, peace-making and peace-keeping. It is worth noting that peacebuilding was not included in the original request of the Security Council, but was added by the Secretary-General on the grounds that it was a closely related concept.

The fact that peacebuilding was largely ignored in 1992 by the political leaders of the UNSC is instructive as to how novel the concept was in political terms at that time. In fact, the report had to justify including peacebuilding by linking it with peace-keeping. It stated that:

> peace-keeping operations, to be truly successful, must come to include comprehensive efforts to identify and support structures which will tend to consolidate peace and advance a sense of confidence and well-being among people.[4]

The report went on to argue that once peace-making and peace-keeping had achieved their objectives (the cessation of hostilities and the maintenance of such a cessation until a peace agreement is reached) the concept of peacebuilding had to come into play as a counterpart to preventive diplomacy. An Agenda for Peace viewed peacebuilding as "sustained, cooperative work to deal with underlying economic, social, cultural and humanitarian problems in order to build peace on durable foundation. Preventive diplomacy is to avoid a crisis; post-conflict peace-building is to prevent a recurrence".

While the report dealt with the concept of peacebuilding in three short pages, its inclusion was critical in raising its profile internationally as well as domestically. Apart from raising the profile of post-conflict peacebuilding amongst decision-makers (and the academic community) An Agenda for Peace highlighted the multifaceted nature of peacebuilding as a concept that addressed itself to the social, economic, cultural and humanitarian dimensions of conflict. The multidimensional nature of post-conflict peacebuilding remains its major characteristic and a major challenge. Over time, the conception of peacebuilding outlined in An Agenda for Peace has been subject to various critiques, such as its top-down approach, its focus on post-conflict peacebuilding (as opposed to peacebuilding actions in any context), etc.[5] Nevertheless, it is important to acknowledge the critical role played by An Agenda for Peace in creating the dynamic that put peacebuilding at the centre of political attention in the 1990s.

This attention at the UN level as well as within other international and regional organisations in turn spawned a substantial outpouring of scholarly literature on peacebuilding. It was remarked in 2015 that "the field of peacebuilding is…potentially vast, and academia has not failed to join the conversation with a rapidly growing body of literature whose works are often written by research analysts straddling the practitioner-scholar divide".[6] This literature reflects the multidimensional character of the concept itself as it covers a multitude of academic disciplines including political science, international relations, development studies, CRP studies as well as more recently international law.

In reality, international law scholars have been late in joining the peacebuilding fray. 2012 marked the 20th anniversary of An Agenda for Peace and by that time the scholarly literature on peacebuilding was already substantial. However, at that stage, international law was largely absent as an academic discipline from the peacebuilding literature, especially when compared to the disciplines of international relations, political science or even development studies.

The reasons for such an absence can only be surmised. The traditional approach of international law to armed conflict dominated by the *jus ad bellum* and *jus in bello* perspectives might have been partly responsible. International legal scholars with an interest in armed conflict primarily dealt with issues concerning humanitarian intervention, international humanitarian law and international criminal law. The relationship between international law and *post bellum* contexts was not at the centre of attention. The issues were not examined and explored principally from a peacebuilding perspective but almost exclusively from legal perspectives (such as whether or not international law was being complied with, how international law was developing and the extent to which rules of law were changing in the various contexts).

For example, following the Bosnian conflict and the Rwandan genocide international lawyers primarily explored development in international criminal law from the perspective of how international criminal law was evolving post the establishment of the Yugoslavia and Rwanda *Ad Hoc* Tribunals. The establishment of the International Criminal Court again produced a plethora of literature (very little of which had a peacebuilding perspective). In the aftermath of the NATO bombing of Serbia in the context of the Kosovo conflict, international law scholars examined the issue of the legality of the bombing in the context of the doctrine of humanitarian intervention. The main focus here was whether the *jus ad bellum* had expanded from the strict confines of the UN Charter. The 1990s were also a period in which international law academia turned more intensely to international human rights law including the application of human rights norms and processes in various settings such as conflict situations, developing countries and international as well as regional tribunals.

In a sense, these branches of international law which concerned themselves with conflict and peace were viewed largely in isolation from the broader perspectives of peacebuilding. This void began to be slowly filled in the 2000s. The 2003 invasion of Iraq by the United States and the United Kingdom and particularly its disastrous aftermath of continued strife and turmoil in Iraq was possibly a catalyst for the international law community to commence a more structured exploration of the relationship between international law and post-conflict peacebuilding.[7] In 2007, Charlesworth wrote a think-piece on the role of international humanitarian law after the war in the context of the occupation of Iraq which highlighted several challenges to the law of occupation in the contemporary world.[8] This piece, however, was limited to one aspect of international humanitarian law and its relevance to the immediate post-conflict phase. In 2009, it was still possible to claim that the international law dimension of peacebuilding "seems to have attracted only little attention among scholars and practitioners".[9]

Indeed, the material produced in the early 2000s was rather narrow in scope. It dealt with particular aspects of international law and post-conflict peacebuilding, such as the law of occupation mentioned above, responses to mass atrocities,[10] the issue of the legal legitimation of state rebuilding in external peacebuilding interventions,[11] feminist perspectives on international law and peacebuilding,[12] etc. A broader conception and examination of an international law of peacebuilding remained largely absent. Even as late as 2011, it was argued that the concept of peacebuilding had been examined and developed by various social science disciplines but not by international law.[13] Nevertheless, by the mid-2000s, international lawyers had finally arrived on the scene and began exploring how various international law dimensions and approaches could contribute to the ongoing debate on peacebuilding.

One may submit that 2008 was an important year in the context of starting the debate around a more holistic approach to the relationship between international law and peacebuilding. Carsten Stahn and Jann Kleffner's edited volume entitled *Jus Post Bellum – Towards a Law of Transition From Conflict to Peace* deserves a special mention as the first academic examination of the origins, contents and contemporary challenges of *jus post bellum*. The book's primary appeal is that it seeks to direct attention to a body of international law which addresses itself to various facets of the peacebuilding machinery that had evolved at that point.

The book is grounded (to some extent) in the old just war tradition and seeks to illustrate that international law has roots upon which to graft the modern emerging law of *jus post bellum*. The first part of the book explores historical roots and theoretical frames. The chapters which address the contents and challenges of the international law of post-conflict transition (the book eschews overall the term international law of peacebuilding) are of greater practical interest. They address selected issues in international law such as the law of occupation, international human rights law, transitional justice issues and matters related to the responsibility to protect. Most of the contributions provide an examination of the then prevailing legal position without offering comprehensive answers to the challenges that existed. As was acknowledged in the preface most contributions "pose the right questions and offer guidance on shortcomings, directions and possible avenues of reform". Most importantly the volume encouraged further exploration of *jus post bellum* and the role of international law in transitioning from war to peace which, the preface again acknowledges "is largely unexplored".

What is also instructive about this volume is that although it is an edited publication with a number of contributors from different disciplines none of them hail from the CRP community. In fact, the three disciplines represented in the volume are philosophy, international law and international relations. The lack of engagement with (or by) CRP scholars/practitioners has thus been a feature of the evolving concept of the international law of peacebuilding from the start.

It is equally instructive to note that the early trajectory of the international law engagement with peacebuilding was greatly influenced by the traditional conceptions and language of international law itself. The main literature on the subject refers to *jus post bellum* so as to both highlight its links with *jus ad bellum* and *jus in bello* but also mark its connection with just war theory (from which the other two branches derive) and continuity with existing international law norms which govern armed conflict. This is an understandable if not automatic, phenomenon as the philosophers and international lawyers involved in the *jus post bellum* undertaking in the late 2000s (and later) relied on the traditions and processes of their respective disciplines in bringing forth the debate around the law that should apply after conflict. This tendency is evident as late as 2021 when an important contribution on the topic was titled *Jus Post Bellum* with a subtitle referring to the rediscovery of the law, with the clear inference of continuity with pre-existing law in this context.[14]

Returning to the evolution of the debates around international law of peacebuilding it is fair to say that it has been largely dominated by a group of international law scholars/practitioners associated with the University of Leiden, which has a long tradition as a centre of excellence in international law. The 2007 volume on *jus post bellum*, which brought a more comprehensive approach to the relationship between international law and post-conflict peacebuilding, was followed in 2014 by another edited volume which sought to continue this debate. *Jus Post Bellum: Mapping the Normative Foundations*[15] edited by Carsten Stahn, Jennifer Easterday and Jens Iverson (all from the University of Leiden's Law School) brought the debate forward in numerous ways.

The volume brought to the fore several important areas for consideration. From a practical perspective, some of the main issues examined are (i) the temporal scope of *jus post bellum* (when does it start to apply and until when), (ii) the relationship between *jus post bellum* and the law of peace agreements, (iii) the relationship to the allied concepts of responsibility to protect and transitional justice, (iv) the application of the relevant norms in interstate conflicts as opposed to intrastate conflicts and (v) the precise contours of the content of the relevant norms (a matter discussed briefly in the previous chapter).

Again, one notes that the volume featured 27 contributors, of which 20 are legal scholars or practitioners. Only one of the contributors could be categorised as belonging to the peace studies community. The extent to which the interface between legal scholars/practitioners and peace and conflict resolution scholar/practitioners remained largely absent in extending the debate around *jus post bellum* is quite manifest in these raw numbers.

The Leiden School continued to play an important role in shaping the debate on international law in post-conflict situations with Jens Iverson's 2021 monograph entitled *Jus Post Bellum: The Rediscovery, Foundations, and Future of the Law of Transforming War into Peace*. The main thrust of this volume is to sustain the belief that *jus post bellum* is indeed a branch of international law, that it is a branch of international law with its roots in the just war tradition and one which has a content that is still evolving and that it is not the same as transitional justice or post-conflict international criminal law *sic et simpliciter*. The author is clear that it is "primarily a work of legal analysis" that also addresses normative issues given the historical roots it has.

These are by no means the only works that have focused on *jus post bellum* since the interest in the law that should apply post-conflict emerged in the late 2000s. However, the three volumes together seem to provide the backbone of the literature on the subject. Overall, there are four broad strands that run through these volumes: (i) the nature of *jus post bellum* and its roots (what is it exactly and what is based upon), (ii) its scope of application (from when and until when does it apply as well as how it applies in different types of conflict), (iii) what are the norms that constitute the body of law that is referred to as *jus post bellum*? and (iv) how *jus post bellum* differs from other related concepts in peacebuilding (such as transitional justice).

The Nature of *Jus Post Bellum* and Its Roots

The main thrust of the existing literature on the nature of *jus post bellum* relies to a considerable degree on its derivation from just war theory. Essentially, the just war tradition requires a legitimate authority to wage war, a just cause for the war as well as rightful intention on the part of those waging war. It is clear that just war theory constitutes an important philosophical underpinning for contemporary international law relating to armed conflict. However, it is important to consider that this conception risks being viewed (and risks being in practice) as an overly Western one. The principal point connecting just war tradition with *jus post bellum* is that the peace that follows the war should itself be just, reflecting the just cause and rightful intention of waging war in the first place. It is evident that the international law of peacebuilding as envisaged in the academic literature referenced thus far has its roots in Western philosophy and theology. It is not rooted in the notions of peacebuilding which emerged since the 1990s and which have been influenced by a broader range of academic disciplines and frameworks (as well as the broader range of voices in terms of both geography and gender).

While an understanding of the just war tradition and how it has shaped existing international rules is relevant, an emphasis on this may also constitute an emphasis on Western philosophic and religious thought. The field of conflict resolution and peacebuilding seeks to involve a multiplicity of perspectives and voices. In view of the above, it is submitted that a conflict resolution/peacebuilding perspective on the international law of post-conflict peacebuilding would rather find its roots in the theory of positive peace referred to in Chapter 1. The conception of positive peace also requires (like just war theory) that the peace that follows violent conflict be just and therefore sustainable. The advantage of using positive peace as a framework for the international law of post-conflict peacebuilding (apart from its appeal to the conflict resolution/peacebuilding community) is that positive peace emphasises *inter alia* issues relating to just relations between individuals and communities, which are especially useful perspectives in the context of non-international armed conflict where communities living within the same nation-state have to repair their relations. The emphasis within positive peace theory on creating structures that assist in managing conflict peacefully and positively further renders this conceptual framework useful in the context of any armed or violent conflict, be it international or internal.

There has been debate on the exact nature of *jus post bellum*. In particular, it has been suggested that it should not be regarded as a positive legal framework but rather as an interpretive framework.[16] At this nascent stage, it seems obvious that presenting the international law of peacebuilding as a positive legal framework is premature. However, there are aspects of it which have an established positive legal framework (such as international human rights law), which while well-established are still amenable to development.

For the purposes of conflict resolution and peacebuilding work, a pragmatic approach to this debate is preferable. In this context, the body of law that constitutes the international law of post-conflict should be viewed as a body or compendium of rules of international law – broadly defined – that should, or may, be applied in post-conflict situations. International law has long recognised (formally at least since the Lotus Case[17]) that its rules may be either mandatory or permissive in nature. The contextual differences in post-conflict situations may be great (international armed conflict as opposed to non-international armed conflict/ethnic conflicts as opposed to conflicts over natural resources or territorial conflicts/conflicts in Europe as opposed to those in Latin America or Africa). Thus, the existence of mandatory and permissive rules of international law allows for both a uniform application of fundamental norms (such as non-discrimination in access to or participation in political life, i.e., the prohibition of apartheid) and contemporaneously the application or otherwise of permissive rules depending on the particular post-conflict context (such as rules relating to internal self-determination as explained below).

Therefore, the international law of post-conflict peacebuilding should be viewed as a collection of rules of international law which, in the case of certain fundamental rules, must be applied in a post-conflict situation while, in the case of other rules, they may be applied as part of the post-conflict peacebuilding settlement. This approach has the advantage of ensuring adherence to universally acknowledged norms such as the prohibition of apartheid, while at the same time permitting the communities impacted by the conflict, their political representatives and peace practitioners (through NGOs, INGOs or academia) to choose which non-fundamental peacebuilding norms to apply.

In this latter case, the application of existing international law rules on self-determination provides a good example. As illustrated in the previous chapter, the current rules on self-determination in international law (apart from lacking absolute clarity) are applicable only in contexts such as foreign domination, occupation and colonial situations. Thus, they would only be clearly applicable in armed conflicts which are characterised by one of these dimensions. However, this is the rule relating to external self-determination, i.e., the creation or re-establishment of a new state (as in the Kosovo case). The law of self-determination also allows for internal self-determination, i.e., the granting of a large degree of political autonomy to a region within an existing state without creating a new state. For example, currently, Scotland remains a part of the United Kingdom but with a high level of self-government and control of most aspects of its internal governance. The application (or not) of this form of internal self-determination will depend on the nature of the conflict as well as the judgment of the conflicting parties as to its practicality in a specific context.

The Scope of Application

The temporal scope of application of *jus post bellum* seems to be apparent in the term itself, i.e., this body of law should apply once the armed conflict has ended. However, determining when a conflict has ended is not always straightforward. This is especially the case of frozen conflicts, such as the situation prevailing in Cyprus. Should the rules of the international law of post-conflict peacebuilding be applicable in Cyprus? The armed conflict in Cyprus was suspended as a result of the ceasefire agreement of 16 August 1974 and the formal position has not changed since then. For some, the situation in Cyprus is still in the peace-making and peace-keeping stage (as evidenced by the continued presence of UN peacekeepers who monitor the buffer zone between the two conflicting parties). For others, the decades of negotiations and progress registered in opening travel between the Republic of Cyprus and Northern Cyprus across the so-called Green Line are all forms of peacebuilding irrespective of the formal status of the conflict.

Moreover, some of the international law rules relating to *jus in bello* (international humanitarian law) may cross over the temporal line between in conflict and post-conflict. This is the case for the law of occupation which is considered part of *jus in bello* but has consequences for peacebuilding in the post-conflict phase. For example, under the international law of occupation, the occupying power/s has the ability to legislate for the occupied territory. As a case in point, one may refer to the various trials of the late 1940s in Germany that were held in terms of laws passed by the Allied Control Council.

The work of Iverson in this context is especially relevant as he eschews a purely temporal approach to the application of *jus post bellum*, i.e., that this branch of law is only applicable once the armed conflict has terminated. The temporal approach argues that the three branches of international law related to armed conflict are applicable in sequence at the beginning, during and after the end of the armed conflict. Iverson instead argues for the adoption of a "hybrid functional" approach where "*jus ad bellum*, *jus in bello*, and *jus post bellum* can overlap temporally, but differ in terms of function".[18] In this view, there may be aspects of *jus post bellum* which are applicable, while the armed conflict is still not completely resolved. This approach has the advantage of resolving the issue of whether *jus post bellum* may be applicable in frozen conflicts such as the Cypriot conflict. Under this "hybrid functional" approach, the international law of post-conflict peacebuilding is applicable in frozen conflicts to the extent that the parties are engaging in peacebuilding initiatives while a permanent solution is still being sought.

The second aspect relating to the scope of application of *jus post bellum* refers to the distinction between international and non-international armed conflicts. In international humanitarian law, the distinction between the two is drawn by referring to the Geneva Conventions of 1949 which distinguish on the basis of whether an armed conflict is between two (or more) parties to the Convention which are by definition states or not. In the latter case, where the armed conflict is between a state and a non-state actor the conflict is characterised as non-international. However, it is important to note that cases of military occupation are also considered international in nature even if the occupied territory is purported to be part of its territory by the occupying power. Moreover, as per Additional Protocol II to the Geneva Conventions of 1977, the international character of armed conflict is also attributed to conflicts where "peoples are fighting against colonial domination and alien occupation and against racist regimes in the exercise of their right of self-determination". In practice, this extends the scope of international armed conflict to include conflicts which are related to situations to which external self-determination is clearly applicable in international law.

In most cases, except for armed conflicts in the context of the right to external self-determination, the distinction between international and non-international armed conflict is based on whether the conflict is between (two or more) states or between a state and one or more non-state actors within the same state. Iverson's detailed examination of the distinction between these two types of armed conflict and the relevance of this distinction for *jus post bellum* is relevant for conflict resolution and peacebuilding practitioners mainly for the conclusion that different rules within the broad body of *jus post bellum* may have greater or lesser relevance depending on what type of conflict is being considered. He summarises this in the following terms:

> resolving non-international conflicts is primarily an issue of what sort of state (or, in the case of secession, states) will be built in the aftermath of war, whereas international armed conflicts inevitably are not only an issue of the post-war nature of the states involved but also the nature of interstate relations afterwards.[19]

Thus, the major relevance of this distinction is that different norms in the corpus of law that constitutes the international law of post-conflict peacebuilding may be applied depending on the nature of the armed conflict and, in particular, on the specific post-conflict context that emerges. Norms of post-conflict peacebuilding that refer to interstate relations will be more relevant in international armed conflicts, while (usually) norms relating to state-building are more relevant in non-international armed conflicts.

The Norms of Post-Conflict Peacebuilding

In Chapter 1, the major branches of international law that constitute the backbone of the international law of peacebuilding were sketched out. The legal norms referred to in Chapter 1 are broadly in-line with the existing literature on *jus post bellum*. An aspect which was not dealt with in Chapter 1 and which is often referenced in the existing literature is the notion of procedural fairness. This refers particularly to the fairness of the process which eventually leads to a peace treaty (for international armed conflicts as only states or international organisations may enter into treaties) or peace agreements (for non-international armed conflicts, given that the generic term agreement may include treaties but also refers to other types of agreement which non-state actors may validly enter into).[20]

Essentially, the key feature of procedural fairness relates to the matter of whether an agreement or treaty was reached without the threat or use of force. Legal scholars refer particularly to article 52 of the Vienna Convention on the Law of Treaties which invalidates any treaty that is concluded consequent to a threat of use of force. By definition, peace treaties are negotiated and entered into as a result of the use of force and thus the question arises as to whether peace treaties observe the requirements of this article. While there may be some academic discussion on this issue it is a matter of record that peace treaties or peace agreements have never been formally invalidated on these grounds. Other issues which are discussed in the context of procedural fairness are likewise related to the conclusion of peace treaties/agreements.

One such issue is the matter of coercion of representatives who sign such treaties/agreements. It is both a matter of treaty law[21] as well as a general principle of law that coercion invalidates a treaty/agreement as it would lack a fundamental character of any agreement, i.e., freely expressed consent to be bound by the rules constituting the agreement. Other elements discussed by Iverson under this rubric of procedural fairness are amnesties and the *aut dedere aut judicare* principle (i.e. a state must either prosecute or surrender/extradite for prosecution persons accused of having committed certain crimes). The matter of amnesties has been alluded to in the previous chapter with the position being that the UN officially, and as a matter of policy, rejects amnesties for the most serious crimes under international law. As a matter of fact, large numbers of individuals who commit these serious crimes (in the context of armed conflict) are not prosecuted.

The *aut dedere, aut judicare* principle is included in a number of widely ratified international treaties (such as the Convention on the Prevention and Punishment of the Crime of Genocide and the Convention Against Torture) that require the prosecution of individuals who commit certain crimes (such as genocide and torture). This principle is, in one sense, a more positive obligation than the prohibition of amnesties (a negative obligation). It requires the prosecution or surrender/extradition of any individual accused of the commission of the relevant crime/s as a matter of international law. States who have ratified these treaties and who fail to fulfil the *aut dedere aut judicare* principle are liable in international law on the basis of state responsibility.

These principles lie at the heart of the "no peace without justice" agenda and the "fight against impunity" which are an important strand of international criminal law. Nevertheless, there are clearly contrasting views in the conflict/peace community on the desirability of entrenching these norms in all post-conflict scenarios. The differences on this matter are returned to in Chapter 4.

The role of international criminal law in conflict resolution and peacebuilding is related to the norms of international human rights law, given that crimes against humanity, one of the four core crimes included in international criminal law, may be defined as grave breaches of international human rights norms committed by or with the consent of a state or an organisation.[22] International human rights law has evolved into a distinct and fully fledged component of international law, with number of international treaties adopted under its umbrella ranging from the rights of the child[23] to economic, social and cultural rights.[24] Moreover, international human rights law covers both global instruments such as the Convention on the Elimination of Discrimination Against Women as well as regional instruments such as the African Charter on Human and People's Rights. It has assumed a significant position within the UN and other international fora as a normative framework that is both constantly reiterated and defined as a pillar of international society. In reality, it is also constantly violated both in peacetime and more so in situations of armed conflict. This latter fact has brought international human rights law within the constellation of conflict resolution and peacebuilding as a relevant consideration.

In the context of conflict resolution and peacebuilding, international human rights law is associated both with direct or physical violence as well as the root causes of conflict in the form of systematic violations of human rights norms against a distinct group.[25] Human rights legal frameworks feature in most peace dispensations. South Africa, Northern Ireland and Colombia are examples of this trend. For these reasons, international human rights law in post-conflict situations has attracted significant scholarly attention both from legal scholars as well as CRP scholars and practitioners. Respect for international human rights law in the 1980s to the early 2000s became a badge of international respectability.[26] The extent to which these frameworks are owned by local actors (including the local peacebuilding community) is a different matter. For Stahn, one of the branches of international law that regulates peace agreements is international human rights law,[27] while Chetail includes international human rights law as one of the components of post-conflict peacebuilding.[28] There is a risk that international human rights frameworks are incorporated without reference to the local conditions and experiences, precisely because international human rights law is a mark of international respectability rather than because the affected community genuinely believe such a framework assists them in moving towards positive peace.

As a counter-point, one may refer to anthropological perspectives on human rights (both generally and specifically within conflict settings) which critique the claims of universality upon which the international human rights legal framework has been constructed since the adoption of the Universal Declaration of Human Rights Mark Goodale, for example, unequivocally refers to "the failure of international human rights – its tribunals, its international bodies, its ethics of naming-and-shaming – to fulfil its apparent destiny…".[29] He calls for a reimagination of human rights based on a principle he refers to as "translocality" rather than universality. That there is a need for a constructive dialectic between these and many other views and positions from legal and other disciplines is clear.

Conclusion

The matters considered in this chapter are relevant from two key dimensions that lie at the heart of this book: (i) what are the main issues that have been discussed in academic literature relating to the international law of post-conflict peacebuilding and (ii) within which academic disciplines or contexts have these issues been discussed. In terms of the first point, it is clear that the academic discussion of this relatively new branch of international law has focused on its historic roots, its nature and scope of application as well as the legal content of its norms. These are matters which CRP scholars and practitioners should be aware of and also engage with in order to shape them.

Thus, the second point, is linked to the first to the extent that this book argues that the CRP community needs to engage more with the development of the international law of peacebuilding. As highlighted earlier in this chapter and as evidenced by the legal jargon permeating the literature, the early evolution of the international law of post-conflict peacebuilding has been led by legal scholars and practitioners with a minor role for political scientists and philosophers (mainly with respect to the roots and nature of *jus post bellum*).

The absence of the CRP community from the discussions on the international law of peacebuilding may be perplexing given this is the area of international law which directly impacts their discipline. However, this lack of engagement is also evident within the CRP scholarly community. As we shall see in Chapter 4, CRP scholars and practitioners have themselves not engaged substantially with international law in general and the international law of peacebuilding in particular. Exploring some of the reasons for this lack of interaction is a question that can generate interesting insights to improve the general cooperative approach between the legal and CRP communities. While the causes are likely numerous, one needs to assess the relationship between legal scholars and practitioners (particularly international lawyers) with CRP scholars and practitioners. The next chapter will address this matter.

Notes

1 Jabri, V. (2016). Post-Colonialism: A Post-Colonial Perspective on Peacebuilding. In *The Palgrave Handbook of Disciplinary and Regional Approaches to Peace*, eds Richmond, O. P., Pogodda, S. and Ramović, J. New York: Palgrave Macmillan:154–167.

2 English, M. D. and Rubenstein, R. E. (2022). Systemic Violence. In *Encyclopedia of Violence, Peace, & Conflict* (3rd edition), ed. Kurtz, L. Oxford: Academic Press: 439.

3 Boutros-Ghali, B. (1992). *An Agenda for Peace: Preventive Diplomacy, Peacemaking and Peace-keeping.* Nations and United Nations and Report of the Secretary General pursuant to the statement adopted at the Summit Meeting of the Security Council on 31 January 1992. 17 June 1992. SC Doc. S/24111. https://www.securitycouncilreport.org/atf/cf/{65BFCF9B-6D27-4E9C-8CD3-CF6E4FF96FF9}/Disarm S24111.pdf

4 United Nations: Report of the Secretary General: para. 21.

5 King, E. and Matthews, R. O. (2012). A new agenda for peace: 20 years later. *International Journal 64,* no.2 (Spring). https://www.jstor.org/stable/23266007

6 Chetail, V. and Jütersonke, O. (2015). Peacebuilding: An Overview of the Academic Literature. *Geneva Peacebuilding Platform White Paper Series*, no. 13. https://papers.ssrn.com/sol3/papers.cfm?abstract_id=2684002

7 Christine Bell has argued that one of the two key drivers of the interest in *jus post bellum* has been North American philosophers who were grappling with the consequences of the US-led military intervention in Iraq and who considered how just war theory might apply to post-international intervention. See Bell, C. Of Jus Post Bellum and Lex Pacificatoria: What's in a Name?. In Stahn and Carsten, *Jus Peace after Conflict.*

8 Charlesworth, H. (2007). Law after War. *Melbourne Journal of International Law* 8 (2): 233.

9 Schaller, C. Towards an International Legal Framework for Post-conflict Peacebuilding.

10 Lambourne, W. (2006). Justice in the Aftermath of Mass Crimes: International Law and Peacebuilding. In *The Challenge of Conflict: International Law* Responds, eds U. Dolgopol and J. Gardma. Leiden: Brill.

11 Oeter, S. (2005). Post-Conflict Peacebuilding – Völkerrechtliche Aspekte der Friedenskonsolidierung in Nachkriegsgesellschaften. *Die Friedens-Warte* 80: 41–60.

12 Chinkin, C. and Charlesworth, H. (2006). Building Women into Peace: The International Legal Framework. *Third World Quarterly* 27: 5.

13 Añaños, M. C. (2011). La consolidación de la paz en el derecho internacional. *Estudios Internacionales* 168: 51–86.

14 Iverson, J. *Jus Post Bellum.*

15 Stahn, C., Easterday, J. S. and Iverson, J. (2014). *Jus Post Bellum: Mapping the Normative Foundations.* Oxford: Oxford University Press.
16 Stahn, Easterday and Iverson. *Jus Post Bellum.*
17 *The Case of S.S. Lotus (France v. Turkey)* (1927) PCIJ (Ser A) No 10.
18 Iverson, J. *Jus Post Bellum:* 10.
19 Iverson, J. *Jus Post Bellum:* 10.
20 The peace process in Northern Ireland is useful in explaining this distinction. The ending of the violence in Northern Ireland involved an agreement between the United Kingdom and Ireland (which is technically a treaty between states) and an agreement between the conflicting parties in Northern Ireland known as the Multiparty Agreement (not a treaty and, in fact, included as an annex to the interstate agreement as it involved non-state actors representing the main communities in Northern Ireland).
21 *Vienna Convention on the Law of the* Treaties, 23 May 1969, Vol. 1155 (entered into force 27 January 1980): Art. 51.
22 The definition of crimes against humanity is found in *Rome Statute of the International Criminal Court,* 17 July 1998 (entered into force 1 July 2002): Art. 7.
23 *United Nations Convention on the Rights of the Child,* 20 November 1989, General Assembly Resolution 44/25 (entered into force 2 September 1990).
24 *International Covenant on Economic, Social and Cultural Rights,* 16 December 1966, General Assembly resolution 2200A (XXI) (entered into force 3 January 1976).
25 Grech, O. (2010). Human Rights and the Conflict Cycle: A Synopsis. In *Human Rights and the Conflict Cycle*, ed. Grech, O. and Wohlfeld, M. Msida: MEDAC.
26 Grech, *Human Rights and the Northern Ireland Conflict*: 237.
27 Stahn, C. (2006). 'Jus ad bellum', 'jus in bello'...'jus post bellum?' – Rethinking the Conception of the Law of Armed Force. *European Journal of International Law* 17 (5): 937.
28 Chetail, V. (2009). Introduction: Post-Conflict Peacebuilding – Ambiguity and Identity. In Post-C*onflict Peacebuilding: A Lexicon,* ed. Chetail, V. Oxford: Oxford University Press: 18.
29 Goodale, M. (2022). *Reinventing Human Rights.* California: Stanford University Press: ix.

3 Lawyers and Peace Practitioners

An Uneasy Relationship

Introduction

This chapter will explore some aspects of the relationship between lawyers and Conflict Resolution and Peace (CRP) practitioners and scholars. While the relationship has been examined in some of the existing literature this has been done mainly in the context of conflict resolution and human rights. The broader relationship between legal practitioners and conflict resolution practitioners has not been, substantially, examined. In this chapter, the exploration of this relationship will be broadened to the relationship between conflict resolvers/peace practitioners and lawyers across the field. The aim of this chapter is to assess whether frictions between the two approaches exist, what they consist of and the underlying reasons for these frictions. Areas of convergence between the praxis of law and conflict resolution/peacebuilding will also be drawn out.

That a perception of friction exists between legal practitioners and conflict resolution/peace practitioners arises especially out of the notorious (and to some extent tedious debate) on the "peace v justice" conundrum. My own experience of this, dates back to postgraduate studies in international law, soon after the adoption of the Rome Statute of the International Criminal Court. The slogan "No Peace Without Justice" was all pervasive, as was the understanding of law students and practitioners that justice could only mean the justice achieved through a judicial organ established to punish individuals guilty of the "most serious crimes of concern to the international community as a whole". The Preamble of the Statute tells us that this punishment of such perpetrators is intended "to guarantee lasting respect for and the enforcement of international justice". Punishing perpetrators was self-evidently the only meaning that "justice" may have. In situations of war, violence and atrocities, justice could only mean a court verdict. What else could it mean?

Only later, through the connection with colleagues who were conflict resolution scholar-practitioners, did my conception of the idea of justice widen. Justice could mean different things at different points in the conflict resolution and peacebuilding journey. This is a theme that shall be returned to later in this

DOI: 10.4324/9781003462248-3

chapter. However, a perception of difference (and perhaps divergence in some ways) between lawyers and conflict resolution practitioners remains.

The reasons that will be adduced to explain these divergences and frictions include differences relating to (i) the methodological approaches to how lawyers and peacemakers/peacebuilders operate, (ii) the values and concepts each profession gives priority to, (iii) divergent views around the meaning of expertise and the role of power between the two disciplines and (iv) approaches towards stereotyping of the "other" profession.

Before proceeding with an exploration of some of these differences, it should be noted that these differences are not absolute, and there can be overlap and collaboration between lawyers and peace practitioners in certain cases. Moreover, both professions play vital roles in the overall landscape of conflict resolution, addressing conflicts from different angles and contexts. The overall argument of this book is that they could do so in a more complementary and effective manner. By exploring some of the underlying differences as well as by pointing to areas of convergence, efforts may be made by both sides to bridge any gaps and improve their collaborative framework.

Methodological Differences

Starting from the methodological differences, the most obvious difference between CRP practitioners and legal practitioners is that lawyers operate primarily (if not exclusively) within a legal framework. Lawyers work within such a framework, applying statutes, regulations and case law to resolve disputes and enforce claims. They emphasise legal rights, obligations and formal processes. This method is underpinned by a way of thinking that is sometimes referred to as "legal thinking" or "thinking like a lawyer". In fact, it has been suggested that this approach is inculcated through legal education as "Law teachers advance 'legal thinking' by teaching their students that everyday thinking is inadequate framework and that images of law held by outsiders are naive".[1] This approach provides both for a belief that there is a mode of thinking, speaking and acting that is connected to and required by the legal framework and secondly, that such mode of thinking, speaking and acting is in some way "superior" to modes of thinking and action by non-lawyers.

CRP practitioners, on the other hand, often utilise transformative processes that go beyond legal considerations and legal frameworks. They engage in mediation, dialogue facilitation and conflict analysis to address the underlying causes of conflict, promote reconciliation and transform relationships. They focus (primarily) not on legal rights and duties but on repairing broken relations. Scholar-practitioners, such as Lederach, emphasise the relational and transformational perspectives within the conflict resolution and peacebuilding domain.[2]

A further methodological difference is that lawyers (particularly those operating within court systems) generally function within an adversarial context and represent one or more distinct clients. Even within mediation or other Alternative Dispute Resolution (ADR) processes, which are not adversarial (or less so), lawyers have a deontological duty to do the best for their client/s. Peace and conflict resolution practitioners base their practice on collaborative processes. Rubenstein and Blecherman state explicitly that many in the CRP community would advocate the avoidance of adversarial approaches as essential to the reach the objectives of conflict resolution:

> Many would also affirm that in order to reach this goal, the sources of violence and contention, which include cultural norms sanctioning or glorifying violence, invidious and discriminatory "isms" (racism, sexism, etc.), gross socioeconomic and political inequities, and **over-reliance on formal, adversarial decision-making procedures need to be eliminated or, at least, mitigated.** (emphasis added)[3]

Within the conflict resolution/peace praxis "approaches to conflict resolution generally call for a non-adversarial framework for addressing the conflict".[4] Moreover, CRP practitioners have peacebuilding as their ultimate goal rather than the interests of a particular client/s.

Lawyers, including human rights lawyers who are heavily involved in conflict resolution and transitional justice settings, typically are trained in and follow an adversarial approach, representing the interests of their clients and aiming to win their case or negotiate the best outcome for them. They emphasise legal rights, rules and where applicable legal precedent. In contrast, CRP practitioners tend to adopt a collaborative approach, seeking to facilitate dialogue and cooperation between conflicting parties. They focus on fostering relationships, building trust and finding mutually beneficial solutions.

Evidently, lawyers typically operate within formal legal processes, such as courts or arbitration settings, which involve strict procedural rules and a predominance of legal professionals. They rely on legal precedent and the application of law. CRP practitioners often employ informal processes, such as problem-solving workshops, dialogue circles, community mediation or restorative justice, which allow for flexibility, inclusivity and community participation. Such settings normally eschew rigid procedures and technical forms. This is in sharp contrast to court settings particularly and legal processes more generally where procedures are at least as important as substantive laws. Suffice it to say that in some jurisdictions the laws of procedure are greater in volume than substantive laws.

Principles and Concepts

Discussing the principles and concepts that the two professions prioritise requires a significant degree of generalisation. While acknowledging the perils of generalisations, it is worth noting that certain principles and concepts form an integral part of the respective profession. It is axiomatic that lawyers have an intrinsic link with the concept of rights. Likewise, CRP practitioners famously focus on interests. Lawyers are trained (and are required as a matter of deontology) to prioritise the legal rights of their clients and aim to protect and enforce these rights. They focus on legal arguments, evidence and litigation strategies.

CRP practitioners, however, focus on the broader interests of the conflicting parties. They explore the underlying needs, desires and concerns of individuals and communities, seeking creative solutions that address those interests and promote sustainable peace. Their primary focus is not on the legally defined rights of the conflicting parties. Since the field of CRP was established as a distinct academic discipline, the focus is on addressing deep-rooted causes of conflict. To the extent that these deep-rooted causes are concerned with an actual or perceived lack of rights, there may be convergence between lawyers and CRP practitioners.

Another conception which often (though not always) differentiates lawyers from CRP practitioners may be termed as the Win-Lose versus Win-Win principle. Lawyers often approach conflict resolution as a win-lose scenario, where one party's victory comes at the expense of the other. Especially in the context of litigation, lawyers strive to maximise their client's advantage and employ tactics to that effect. In such court settings, a lawyer is expected to act in a manner which maximises the client's advantage at the expense of the opposing party/ies. While this approach is not absolute, as in corporate negotiations and other types of negotiations led by lawyers, a win-win scenario is actively sought by the parties, it remains the case that lawyers are generally acting for one party and have a duty to act in their interest within the law.

In contrast, CRP practitioners aspire to achieve win-win outcomes, where both parties benefit and feel their interests are adequately addressed. They emphasise cooperation, collaboration and finding common ground. An essential aspect of peace work is that of building relationships between the conflicting parties, which is not necessarily an integral component of a lawyer's toolbox. Within peace practice, the idea of maximising the advantages to one side over the other is anathema. According to Katz and McNulty, effective resolution of conflict is based on collaboration understood as:

> A win/win strategy based on problem solving where the interests of all parties can be met. This approach results in maintaining strong interpersonal or intergroup relationships while ensuring that all parties achieve their interests.[5]

A further distinction in terms of the principles which the professions prioritise, it is pacific that lawyers in terms of dispute resolution favour the adoption of legal remedies. Lawyers thus primarily focus on legal remedies, such as compensation, injunctions or other types of court orders. The redress of grievances is viewed in terms of the tools which the legal system generally, and the court system particularly, makes available to them. Conversely, CRP practitioners take a more holistic approach, considering the social, economic, cultural and psychological dimensions of conflict. They promote long-term reconciliation, social healing and structural changes to prevent future conflicts. While this thus not exclude remedial action such as compensation, the remedy is not usually seen in punitive terms. This distinction is particularly evident in discussions surrounding the legacy of mass atrocities committed during armed conflict. Lawyers emphasise the role of tribunals and international criminal law to redress the grievances of the victims. CRP practitioners are more likely to consider a range of tools such as truth commissions, other reconciliation processes and alternative – as well as autochthonous – justice mechanisms, such as restorative justice.

The role of rights may also represent a point of divergence between the two professions. Lawyers typically emphasise the rights and legal entitlements of their clients. They focus on protecting and advancing their clients' rights and interests within the legal framework. CRP practitioners are more attuned to an interest-based approach, aiming to identify the needs, concerns and aspirations of all parties involved. This is not to say that they deny that rights play a role in conflict resolution. Although, as is well-known, the conflict resolution field since its inception has focused more on the language of human needs rather than rights.[6] Overall, CRP practitioners seek to find common interests and work towards mutually beneficial agreements that address the underlying interests and needs of all stakeholders and not just the rights of one or more of the conflict participants.

The approach to timeframes may differ too. Lawyers often have to focus on resolving immediate legal disputes and obtaining favourable outcomes within a defined timeframe. Their primary concern is the case at hand and the legal rights of their clients. The cliche that justice delayed is justice denied has such currency that it has been incorporated into domestic and international legal frameworks (at least in terms of criminal law procedures) under the rubric of the right to a fair trial within a reasonable time. The insistence, by human rights advocates, on trials as soon as practicable for perpetrators of mass atrocities is another manifestation of this posthaste temporal approach. This issue is one that shall be returned to in the next chapters.

CRP practitioners are more prone to take a long-term perspective, recognising that conflicts have deep-rooted causes and complex dynamics. They work for sustainable peace and address the structural and systemic issues that contribute to conflicts, seeking to prevent their recurrence. In doing so, they generally understand that their endeavours require long, ill-defined or even unknowable timeframes. Lederach, for example, urges those involved in peacebuilding to think of it in terms of decades not months/years.[7] The dialectic between peace and justice at the heart of some of the debates in the context of post-conflict peacebuilding is an example of a locus where a longer timeframe is advocated by CRP practitioners as one possible way out of the conundrum.

Another distinction between the two professions relates to the notion of authority, expertise and particularly the importance attached to different kinds of expertise. It has been suggested that "law and legal discourse are prototypes of a discourse of authority".[8] This implies a belief in law and legal discourses being both signs of authority that require respect, adherence and deference. The authority to argue, interpret and adjudicate is in this context, is reserved for those with legal training and expertise. Thus, at least in American and European legal traditions (and those influenced by them), it may be claimed that "[L]awyers have a long-standing monopoly over the business of law, and have generally believed that this business belongs exclusively to lawyers".[9]

CRP practitioners have a different approach to authority and expertise. Because the field of CRP studies emerged from various intersecting disciplinary approaches it has been infused from the start with an appreciation for diverse sources of expertise.

By definition, lawyers are expected to possess legal expertise. They specialise, practically exclusively, in legal expertise and use their knowledge of laws, regulations, and precedent to protect and promote the interests of their clients. Lawyers tend to focus on developing specific skills such as the ability to analyse and interpret legal texts and the capacity to build persuasive arguments while presenting them attractively in writing and orally. Because lawyers primarily work with other lawyers (both as colleagues and as opposing counsel), they are less likely to have experience of working collaboratively with professionals coming from disparate professions such as psychology or anthropology. In fact, in the US context, it has been suggested that "power-sharing with non-lawyers is neither a familiar nor comfortable experience for American lawyers".[10]

Conversely, CRP practitioners often employ an interdisciplinary approach that draws on various fields such as psychology, sociology, political science and anthropology. They consider the social, cultural and psychological dimensions of conflicts and work towards holistic solutions that address the underlying causes. To this extent, CRP practitioners tend to come from a wide variety of backgrounds. This is perhaps best illustrated by examining the academic background of those teaching lawyers and CRP practitioners, respectively, at the university level.

As an illustration one can refer to the teaching faculty at two schools within the same university in the United States. George Mason University in Virginia provides a good case study. It is a public university which hosts the oldest and largest conflict resolution/peace school in the United States (the Carter School for Peace and Conflict Resolution) as well as the highly rated Antonin Scalia Law School, which in recent years has been ranked at the top of the Virginia and Washington DC law schools. Of the full-time faculty at the Carter School at the time of writing, there are two historians, two social psychologists, one lawyer, four peace and conflict scholars, three political scientists, two anthropologists, one theologian and one sociologist, while the Dean is an engineer turned peace scholar. As one would expect, the faculty at the Scalia Law School is less varied in terms of professional backgrounds. Out of the 42 full-time faculty, only three do not possess an academic background in law (Juris Doctor or similar) with two being economists and one being a specialist in government policy.

This s not a criticism of either profession. However, it is clear that a mono-professional expertise in law, as opposed to the multifarious professional approaches in peace and conflict studies, must impact on how lawyers and CRP practitioners approach issues or, as a minimum, on the level of experience they possess in terms of interdisciplinary work.

This is evident, *inter alia*, in approaches to language and power. In her book on legal education and language, Elisabreth Mertz discussed the tension between legal language and everyday language. Mertz demonstrates how law students are taught to adopt and employ a distinct legal language, with its technical terminology and formalistic structure, which creates barriers to effective communication between legal professionals and the general public. In the same context, Mertz also explores the hierarchical nature of legal language and its role in maintaining professional boundaries and power dynamics within the legal profession. In effect, Mertz argues that law schools use language to create a sense of authority and expertise amongst faculty and students, reinforcing the professional identity of lawyers and their power as against non-lawyers.

Conversely, peace and conflict resolution places a premium on inclusivity and multidisciplinarity and openness, as evidenced by its pedagogy which calls for an engagement with its rich multidisciplinarity "especially given the multiple origins of the field's current trajectories".[11] This attitude of "deep commitment to interdisciplinarity and to multidisciplinarity"[12] is an essential component of peace and conflict studies as well as its practice.

Ideas on Justice

It is clear that conceptions of justice differ even amongst lawyers and amongst CRP practitioners themselves. However, as alluded to in the introduction to this chapter, the concept of legal justice is one which is important in this context. This conception of justice is founded on the proper application and interpretation of the law. It holds that justice is achieved when legal rules and principles are followed, ensuring that individuals are treated fairly and consistently according to the established legal framework. This perspective emphasises the importance of due process, equal treatment under the law and adherence to legal procedures. In this sense, it is closely related to the "rule of law", which for a significant number of lawyers represents the fundamental defence against the exercise of arbitrary power.[13]

Another conception of justice amongst lawyers is rooted in corrective measures and may be termed as corrective justice. Lawyers may see justice as a means of correcting wrongs and restoring balance or fairness. This perspective focuses on compensation for harm caused, punishment for wrongdoing and restoring the injured party to their original position. It often involves seeking remedies through litigation or other legal processes. Legal justice is also related to procedural justice emphasizing the fairness and transparency of legal processes themselves. This conception is underpinned by the belief that justice is achieved when individuals have the opportunity to present their case, challenge evidence and have their disputes resolved through a fair and impartial process. This perspective is concerned with ensuring that the procedures followed are just, regardless of the outcome. In sum, lawyers mostly engage with what are termed as procedural justice and corrective/retributive justice.

CRP practitioners base their work on resolving the underlying or root causes of conflict. In this context, through the work of scholars such as John Burton, it has become clear that often these root causes are related to or derived from systemic or structural forms of violence. This approach to CRP work has become a mainstream one. It clearly intersects with the principles of social justice by addressing structural inequalities, promoting equal access to basic needs, recognising and including diverse perspectives and facilitating participatory decision-making. Within the CRP field, the work of Morton Deutsch on distributive justice was an early and strong influence on the relationship between justice and conflict.[14] In particular, ideas on the relationship between distributive justice and conflict have long-infused views on how social justice intersects with conflict resolution.

Another conception of justice often favoured in this context is restorative justice as developed inter alia by Howard Zehr. This conception of justice is based on a commitment to repair the harm done and repair the relation between the victim and perpetrator. An approach which focuses on meeting unmet needs and addressing underlying causes of conflicts, aligns with the principles of restorative justice. Likewise, the restorative justice perspective is conducive to the conflict transformation model which Lederach proposes with its emphasis on the relational aspects of individuals and communities. One may also add that by seeking to restore justice and dignity to individuals and communities affected by conflicts, this approach contributes to social justice goals.

Here it is worth noting that these different conceptions of justice should not be seen as necessarily mutually exclusive. Nor are most CRP practitioners prone to state that legal conceptions of justice are wrong. However, they may be seen as incomplete or insufficient from a conflict resolution and peacebuilding perspective. A way of presenting the difference is by conceiving of justice as a toolbox. Generally, lawyers tend to focus on fewer of these tools when compared to CRP practitioners.

While lawyers and CRP practitioners may approach conflict resolution differently, there can be instances where their approaches intersect.

For example, lawyers may employ mediation techniques to facilitate settlement negotiations, or peace practitioners may utilise legal frameworks to enforce agreements. Examples of this include the use of mediation in matrimonial legal disputes, which has become pervasive. Likewise, peace agreements are usually cast in legal form. Moreover, the same agreements may incorporate or reference legal provisions derived from existing regional or international norms.[15] In sum, it seems that collaboration between these two disciplines may serve to enhance the effectiveness of conflict resolution efforts. We now turn to the field of ADR as a potential locus for developing more collaborative and complementary relations between lawyers and non-lawyers in the context of conflict resolution practice.

Alternative Dispute Resolution – A Meeting Point?

The field of ADR may be seen as fertile ground for lawyers and CRP practitioners to intersect. This is so because ADR is the first field where (at least) in the Western legal tradition, lawyers and non-lawyers have practiced in the same professional field for some time.

As suggested above, lawyers have traditionally been sceptical of sharing the legal profession with non-lawyers. Legal education has not had a strong tradition of interdisciplinarity and lawyers' experiences in this context remain limited. These limited experiences are nevertheless increasing. It has become more common for lawyers working in family litigation to work with psychologists or allied professionals, while corporate lawyers regularly work with finance experts and auditors. Similarly, criminal lawyers are used to working with forensic experts in trial settings. However, in these contexts, lawyers are often not so much working with persons who possess different expertise. They are more likely to be utilising their respective expertise while retaining control of the legal dimension.

Nevertheless, it has been argued that while the rise of ADR has provoked some changes to traditional approaches taken by lawyers it is also the case that these changes have met with some resistance – as previously indicated. This is probably true of American and European lawyers and other jurisdictions where the adversarial system inherent in courts and tribunals prevails. Notwithstanding remaining diffidence, the role of ADR and specifically of mediation as a space for connecting lawyers and other professionals as well as law with other disciplines deserves attention:

> The ADR movement, and mediation in particular, offers the legal profession a different view of access to the law and, in the process, an expansion of the law's ambit.[16]

Notwithstanding the indubitable challenges, ADR processes, such as mediation, may still provide a useful meeting point for lawyers and CRP practitioners to work together and learn from each other. As one of the most widely utilised ADR mechanisms, it is worthwhile examining briefly the main tenets of mediation which will serve to explore the extent to which collaboration and mutual learning may occur in the mediation context. The first essential tenet is that mediation involves a neutral third party (or parties), the mediator, who assists parties in resolving their conflicts through open communication, negotiation and collaboration.

The premise on which mediation is based is that it is a voluntary process in which participants willingly engage and have the freedom to make decisions about the outcome. This is clearly distinct from resolving disputes through litigation, where a party may force the other to submit to court proceedings. The key actor in the mediation process is not the judge or the legal counsels to the litigating parties but a neutral and impartial mediator. The role of the mediator is that of facilitating communication between the parties and helping them identify and understand each other's interests and needs. The mediator, unlike lawyers in litigation, does not represent one of the sides but assists both sides in an impartial manner. Primarily the mediator seeks to assist both parties in finding mutually acceptable solutions rather than providing a final determination. Unlike a judge, a mediator does not impose decisions but supports the parties in finding their own solutions.[17]

Mediation provides a less formal setting compared to traditional litigation. The process can adapt to the parties' needs and allows for flexibility in scheduling, location and the format of the sessions. This informality helps foster a cooperative atmosphere and is a less intimidating environment than courtrooms. As a practical example, mediations are usually not held in court buildings while the timings and dates of the mediation sessions are normally agreed to between the parties. Litigation is conducted in courtrooms while the timing and dates lie within the discretion of the judge. All of these matters are illustrative of a different approach with formality and authority being replaced with informality and shared responsibility.

Mediation encourages parties to explore and articulate their underlying interests and needs rather than taking rigid positions. Although it is important to remind ourselves that even amongst the CRP community there are different approaches to mediation and views on the role of mediator.[18] By understanding each other's motivations, parties can work together to find creative solutions that address their concerns effectively.[19] A further key characteristic of mediation is that it emphasises effective communication and active listening skills. The mediator facilitates dialogue, ensuring that each party has an opportunity to express their perspective, while also encouraging respectful and constructive communication between the parties.[20] A further fundamental distinction between litigation and mediation is that the latter always seeks to achieve mutually beneficial outcomes where both parties feel satisfied (win-win solutions referred to earlier). The focus is on generating solutions that address the interests of all parties involved, promoting a cooperative mindset instead of a win-lose mentality.[21]

A corollary of the win-win mentality is that this assists in preserving or restoring relationships. Mediation recognises the importance of preserving relationships, particularly in situations where ongoing interactions between parties are desired or necessary. By providing a non-adversarial environment (as opposed to the adversarial process in litigation), mediation aims to foster understanding and promote long-term cooperation.[22]

Lawyers practicing mediation, and who internalise these aspects of mediation, may be best placed to understand the cooperative, non-adversarial, informal and empowering nature of conflict resolution and peacebuilding practice. To the extent that it allows lawyers to escape from rigid, adversarial processes mediation may be indeed a useful meeting point for lawyers to recognise the possibilities offered by other approaches such as those used widely in CRP practice.

In the context of ADR, the concept of equity also deserves consideration as a potential meeting point between lawyers and non-lawyers. Equity plays a role in certain aspects of legal practice (both domestic law and international law), including within arbitration. In international law, the role of equity is evident in the Statute of the International Court of Justice which provides that parties to a dispute may allow the Court to determine the dispute on the basis of equity or as Article 38 (2) of the Statute of the Court describes it *ex aequo et bono.*

The notion of equity is an amorphous one that is prone to be interpreted in different ways, with different meanings assigned in various domestic laws. In Anglo-Saxon legal systems, equity has a specific technical meaning, quite distinct from the meaning in international law. In its essence, it bears a commonality with the meaning given to equity more generally, in that it is a branch of law that seeks to provide remedies in situations where statutory provisions might not apply or be equitable. The essential aspect of equity in international law and in arbitral settings is that the body making a determination[23] or adjudication between rival claims is not guided exclusively – or even principally – by specific legal provisions but primarily by the principle of fairness. It can be said that, generally, equity in international law and in arbitration seeks to connect more closely law with the idea of justice as fairness. It has been suggested that:

> In general terms, one may say that justice implies fairness, impartiality, equality of treatment, whereas law's function is to ensure order and security in a certain community, taking into consideration several elements, including justice. Equity may be viewed as measures intended to reduce the gap between law and justice in a specific case.

In fact, the International Court of Justice has stated that "equity as a legal concept is a direct emanation of the idea of justice" and equally revealingly that "the legal concept of equity is a general principle directly applicable as law".[24] This latter point that views equity as a potential source of international law is another point of intersection between fairness and law which should be highlighted.

As such, equity as a principle in international law with its connotation of non-technical application of principles of fairness, justice and equitable outcomes may be an attractive crossroads for lawyers and non-lawyers to meet upon.

It would be beneficial for lawyers involved in conflict resolution and peacebuilding efforts (including – and especially – those who specialise in international human rights law in post-conflict societies) to explore and engage with ADR mechanisms including mediation and arbitration (and the concept of equity), with a view to expanding the repertoire and range of experiences with non-lawyers and in non-formal and non-legalistic processes. In the context of peacebuilding, lawyers practising or working within international law are a specific class of lawyers who merit a brief but distinct reference.

International Law, Lawyers and CRP Practitioners

Given that the international law of peacebuilding operates within the ambit of international law rather than domestic law, it is appropriate to consider whether international law provides a more (or less) favourable context for the relationship between lawyers and CRP practitioners. International law mainly governs relations between states and, as such, is a different kind of law from domestic law. In domestic law, the subjects of law owe allegiance to the state and are not sovereign entities. In international law, the legal system attempts to regulate sovereign entities, which do not owe allegiance to any superior supranational authority. Thus, while domestic law is usually centralised, with the state itself being the ultimate source of legal rules and their enforcement, the same cannot be said in the case of international law.[25]

International law rules are derived from a number of sources (treaties and customary international law being the primary ones) and their enforcement mechanisms are diffuse and less direct than in domestic law. The emanation of legal rules is the result of negotiations between states in the case of treaty law and state practice in the case of customary law. The enforcement mechanisms are varied and less clearly defined. Enforcement relies on a number of pressure points such as self-interest, global public opinion, self-defence as well as various types of sanctions (which may be economic, political or military and which may be adopted on a bilateral or multilateral basis). Courts and tribunals also play a different role in international law than they do in domestic law. For a start, states are not automatically subject to the jurisdiction of international courts and tribunals but rather willingly submit to their jurisdiction. If they do not, then by and large they may not be made to submit to an international tribunal's jurisdiction. Once such international courts and tribunals pass judgment, the enforcement of such judgment faces the same challenges of enforcement as rules of international law do. While, in most cases, judgments are adhered to, some are never enforced.

Due to all of these reasons, international lawyers are a somewhat different type of lawyers from those practising exclusively within domestic jurisdictions. The difference emanates from the obvious fact that they work on a different legal plane and are used to more diverse sources of rules and less efficient enforcement mechanisms. To the extent that international law is a more decentralised legal system, international lawyers and CRP practitioners should find more common ground to meet upon. Moreover, the different notions of enforcement in international law should also, in principle, appeal more to the CRP practitioners.

However, this potential convergence in theory has not been particularly noticeable in practice. This lack of concrete convergence may be related to the content of the legal rules which have been developed over time. Some of these have been alluded to in the previous chapters. The prohibition of annexation or recognition of situations brought about by the use of armed force, the rise of international criminal law or the rules on self-determination are all examples of international law rules, which CRP practitioners may have reservations about from the vantage point of their discipline and methodologies.

While acknowledging these differences, one must also point out that international law has also recognised the importance of ADR methods of resolving conflictual situations. In the case of international law, these ADR methods were alternative not only to litigation (as in domestic law) but more pertinently to war, which until the early twentieth century was a main dispute resolution method for interstate disputes. In this context, international litigation is itself one alternative to war. The establishment of the Permanent Court of International Justice in 1919 (and its successor, the International Court of Justice in 1945) was part of this effort. The same may be said of the establishment of the League of Nations in 1919, whereby part of the international community sought to avoid war through the establishment of a permanent intergovernmental institution devoted to the maintenance of international peace.

The UN obviously is a similar effort and, in its Charter, there are specific references to dispute settlement mechanisms. In Article 1, the Charter stipulates that one of its aims is "to bring about by peaceful means, and in conformity with the principles of justice and international law, adjustment or settlement of international disputes or situations which might lead to a breach of the peace". The means through which the UN is mandated to discharge this aim are established in Chapters 6 and 7 of the same Charter. Chapter 6 lists the "pacific means" of dispute settlement while Chapter 7 is devoted to non-pacific means (i.e. military and non-military sanctions).

Article 33 in Chapter 6 provides a list of options which include judicial and non-judicial means of dispute settlement, including ADR mechanisms such as negotiation and mediation:

1 The parties to any dispute, the continuance of which is likely to endanger the maintenance of international peace and security, shall, first of all, seek a solution by negotiation, enquiry, mediation, conciliation, arbitration,

judicial settlement, resort to regional agencies or arrangements, or other peaceful means of their own choice.

2 The Security Council shall, when it deems necessary, call upon the parties to settle their dispute by such means.

Thus, already in 1945 international law itself was acknowledging that ADR should be an integral component of international dispute settlement. To this extent, it is regrettable that greater efforts were not undertaken to utilise these ADR methods in a cooperative context between international lawyers and CRP practitioners. The need to strengthen this aspect of the UN's work has been reiterated at regular intervals by the UN General Assembly. In 2010, a Group of Friends on Mediation was established at the UN with the mission of "promoting a culture of mediation in their national policies, as well as regionally and internationally".[26] Since 2011, the UN General Assembly has issued regular calls for enhancing mediation and good offices within the structures of the UN.[27] Likewise, various UN review processes, such as the report of the High-level Independent Panel on Peace Operations, the report of the Secretary-General on the future of United Nations peace operations as well as the report of the Advisory Group of Experts on the Review of the Peacebuilding Architecture, all called for a stronger emphasis on mediation within the UN.

It would seem that these efforts should provide international law practitioners and CRP practitioners an opportunity to engage in collaborative efforts of the kind this study is advocating. However, there are also limitations within the UN mediation framework that have limited progress in this context. Firstly, the UN's actual utilisation of mediation has not been extensive and successes are even less so. Notwithstanding the calls for an increased focus on mediation. Secondly, the UN system is still largely state-centric and infused with a degree of formality and procedure, which sits uneasily with the ethos of ADR. Thirdly and relatedly, the UN approaches to mediation continue to focus on officials whether they be national diplomats or legal experts or the equivalent within the UN system. All of this limits the extent to which informal, open and non-legalistic spaces of ADR may fully flourish as a locus for a collaborative spirit and mutual recognition between international lawyers and CRP practitioners.

Conclusion

It is evidently impossible to do justice to the relationship between lawyers and CRP practitioners in a brief chapter. Nevertheless, it is important to start intensifying the conversation around how this relationship has evolved, and more importantly how it may be developed and improved. Beyond the field of mediation, academic literature on this relationship appears to be very scant indeed. This, in itself, may indicate the lack of connectivity between the two professions. It should be, as a minimum, a matter of interest to lawyers involved in conflict resolution and peacebuilding settings as well as to CRP practitioners who will have to engage with lawyers in the context of negotiations, peace agreements and peacebuilding processes such as building institutional capacity in realms such as the judiciary and rule of law, policing, security sector reform, legacy of mass atrocities, etc.

The chapter highlights and summarises what seem to be the main divergences in the methodological and conceptual approaches to resolving conflicts between lawyers and CRP practitioners. Naturally, the extent of the divergences will depend on numerous factors, not least the personality of the lawyers and CRP practitioners involved. The personal experiences of practising law in certain fields (e.g. family law as opposed to criminal law) is another important factor. As is the experience or otherwise, of CRP practitioners in working with legal practitioners.

Peace and conflict resolution as a discipline is by definition multidisciplinary. It has, almost inherently, a predisposition for integrating disciplines within it. It can and should take initiatives to analyse the relationship between lawyers and other professionals involved in conflict resolution as well as design processes through which the relationship may develop successfully. Legal practitioners need to make an effort to be less protective of "the law" in terms of the actors who are involved in its development, interpretation and implementation. As lawyers, we should not only welcome but actively seek opportunities to work cooperatively with other professionals whether in courts, mediation, negotiation, problem-solving workshops and particularly for the purposes of this book in shaping a better normative framework for the building of peace.

Notes

1 Elkins, J. R. (1996). Thinking Like a Lawyer: Second Thoughts. *Mercer Law Review* 47, (2).
2 See, for example, Lederach, J. P. (1998). *Building Peace: Sustainable Reconciliation in Divided Societies*. Washington: United States Institute for Peace Press.
3 Rubenstein, R. E. and Bleckman, F. O. (1999). Conflict Resolution and Distributive Justice: Reflections on the Burton Laue-Debate. *Peace and Conflict Studies* 6, (1).
4 Fisher, R. and Kelman, H. (2003). *Conflict Analysis and Resolution*. Oxford: Oxford University Press.
5 Katz, N. And McNulty, K. (1994). Conflict Resolution. Maxwell School of Citizenship and Public Affairs. https://www.maxwell.syr.edu/docs/default-source/ektron-files/conflict-resolution-neil-katz-and-kevin-mcnulty.pdf?sfvrsn=4de5d71e_9
6 See, for example, Burton, J. (1990). *Conflict: Human Needs Theory*. London: Palgrave Macmillan.
7 Lederach, J. P. *Building Peace*: 81.
8 Elkins, J. R. *Thinking Like a Lawyer*.
9 Nolan-Haley, J. (2002). Lawyers, Non-Lawyers and Mediation: Rethinking the Professional Monopoly from a Problem-Solving Perspective. *Harvard Negotiation Law Review* 235.
10 Nolan-Haley. Lawyers, Non-Lawyers and Mediation.

11 Hirsch, S. F. and Paczyńska, A. (2024). *Teaching Peace and Conflict Studies: Engaged Learning and Inclusive Theory*. Cheltenham: Edward Elgar Publishing.
12 Hirsch and Paczyńska. *Teaching Peace and Conflict Studies*.
13 For a full discussion on the rule of law see Bingham, T. (2011). *The Rule of Law*. New York: Penguin Books.
14 Deutsch, M. (1985). *Distributive Justice: A Social-Psychological Perspective*. New Haven: Yale University Press.
15 For example, the Good Friday Agreement of 1998 which ended the violent conflict in Northern Ireland references the European Convention on Human Rights and is underpinned by a treaty between the United Kingdom and Ireland.
16 Nolan-Haley. Lawyers, Non-Lawyers and Mediation.
17 Moore, C. W. (2014). *The Mediation Process: Practical Strategies for Resolving Conflict*, 4th ed. New Jersey: Jossey-Bass.
18 Rubenstein and Bleckman describe the different views on the role of the mediator espoused by two early scholar-practitioners in conflict resolution: John Burton and Jim Laue. They observe that

> Jim operated as if he were a lawyer with both sides as his clients. John's view of third-party facilitation was also activist, but his technique was closer to that of the therapist who distances himself from the client in order to focus attention on the analysis of underlying systemic problems.

19 Fisher, R., Ury, W. and Patton, B. (1991). *Getting to Yes: Negotiating Agreement Without Giving In*. New York: Penguin Books
20 Moore. *The Mediation Process*.
21 Fisher, Ury and Patton. *Getting to Yes*.
22 Moore. *The Mediation Process*.
23 Ladipoth, R. (2017). Equity in International Law, Proceedings of the Annual Meeting. *American Society of International Law* 81: 139.
24 Continental Shelf Case (*Tunisia v Libyan Arab Jamahriya*), Judgement, February 24 1982, ICJ Rep 18.
25 For an exposition of the decentralised nature of international law see inter alia Gaeta, P., Visuals J. E. and Zappalá, S. (2020). *Cassese's International Law*. Oxford: Oxford University Press.
26 See United Nations Peace Maker. Group of Friends of Mediation. https://peacemaker.un.org/networks/group-of-friends
27 See inter alia Resolution adopted by the General Assembly on Strengthening the role of mediation in the peaceful settlement of disputes, conflict prevention and resolution, July 28 2011, A/RES/65/283 and Resolution adopted by the General Assembly on Strengthening the role of mediation in the peaceful settlement of disputes, conflict prevention and resolution, September 9 2016, A/RES/70/304.

4 The International Law of Peacebuilding and the CRP Community

Introduction

This chapter will focus on the views of CRP scholars and practitioners as to the international law of peacebuilding. The question asked in this chapter is what are the views of the conflict and peace communities on issues that may inform or impact the international law of peacebuilding? It will primarily be based on an examination of the views of leading scholar-practitioners as expressed in their writings as well as conversations held with CRP scholars and practitioners.

The communities in question are composed of a wide variety of actors. These actors include individuals who are active in local NGOs working on conflict resolution and peacebuilding projects at community, regional and national levels; employees of international governmental and non-governmental organisations working in the same field; as well as scholars and scholar-practitioners in the peace and conflict studies sector, who work both within local and international organizations. It should also be noted that while a small minority have a legal background, the majority do not. The academic or professional background of those active or working in the conflict resolution/ peacebuilding communities may, of course, impact the knowledge of and views about legal frameworks in post-conflict situations.

The issues that will be explored in this chapter are several but interconnected: (i) the extent to which conflict resolution and peace communities engage with the international law of peacebuilding in practice and in the academic literature they produce, (ii) how may one gauge their attitude to such a legal framework in the context of peacebuilding work and (iii) what insights may their work on conflict resolution and peacebuilding provide in terms of informing and shaping the emerging legal framework.

By exploring these questions, this chapter will serve to chart some key areas of intersection, contrast and connection between the international legal practitioners who have so far dominated the shaping of the international law of peacebuilding and the CRP scholar-practitioners. It will also serve to highlight any areas where cooperation is more likely.

DOI: 10.4324/9781003462248-4

It is self-evident that the views of a select number of scholars and practitioners should not form the basis of definite and far-reaching generalisations. However, together with the existing literature on each discrete question, these views may point the way towards a useful path for the further development of the international law of peacebuilding.

CRP Scholars and Practitioners and the International Law of Peacebuilding: Imperfect Understandings?

One of the most striking features of an examination of the main literature on conflict resolution and peacebuilding (specifically the major textbooks and handbooks) is the limited space they devote to international law. The same may be said for scholars and practitioners who work in CRP from outside the legal community. A scholar-practitioner who works in peacebuilding frankly expressed the view that international law was not a central discipline for peacebuilding. Instead, it fell in the same category as development studies as a discipline that was ancillary to peacebuilding.[1]

This approach is reflected inter alia in one of the main textbooks from which conflict resolution students have studied for the past two decades: Ramsbotham, Woodhouse and Miall's *Contemporary Conflict Resolution*. The 500-page textbook has around a dozen references to international law. There is a reference to Christine Bell's work on Peace Agreements and international law, which relates primarily to peacemaking, while there are also references to the UN Charter and UN peacemaking. Further references to international law are found in the context of the war on terror, where international human rights law (IHRL) is referred to. The main references to international law are found in a short subsection entitled "Conflict Resolution and International Law". In this section, international law is viewed as a force that may contribute towards what the authors term cosmopolitan conflict resolution, but the scope and potential for CRP to shape international law is not really addressed. In a trite phrase, this section explores briefly aspects of what international law can do for CRP, but not what CRP can do for the evolution of international law.

In this context, the authors refer to "cosmopolitan conflict resolution" as "an approach that is not situated within any particular state, society, or established site of power but rather, promotes constructive means of handling conflict". This approach if engaged with by those working on the international law of peacebuilding may engender the thought that we should also consider that the framework of *jus post bellum* is not located within one professional or academic discipline but rather should derive its tenets from several disciplines and professions.

This paucity of substantive engagement with international law is even more evident in Coleman, Deutsch and Marcus' *The Handbook of Conflict Resolution*, which has virtually no references to international law bar for a couple of mentions of the International Criminal Court and International

Humanitarian Law. This is again indicative of the approach to international law within the CRP mainstream scholars and practitioners. CRP scholars, who were instrumental in the evolution of the field – such as Burton, Galtung, Mitchell, Lederach, Avruch and Rubenstein – likewise have not engaged with international law in a sustained or detailed manner. Overall, the general literature on CRP does not focus on international law and views it as a sideshow and not a protagonist. This, in some ways, mirrors the lack of engagement with CRP practitioners by legal scholars working on the international law of peacebuilding agenda, alluded to in Chapter 1. Particularly striking is the fact that while one may identify some references to international law generally or specific aspects of it in the aforementioned CRP literature, references to the international law of peacebuilding and the literature around it are not easily found.[2]

A notable and welcome exception to the dearth of attention devoted to international in the CRP literature is Lester Kurtz's *Encyclopedia of Violence Peace and Conflict*, which in Volume 1 includes an entry on International Law authored by Richard Falk,[3] who himself is an exception to the general lack of international lawyers engaging in a sustained and systematic manner with the CRP community. Falk calls for the "reimagining" of the relationship between law and war and especially engages with the need to re-examine the underlying structure of international law as a system (a matter which is elaborated upon below).

It is also worth noting that even talking to individuals working in international governmental and non-governmental organisations, the conception of the international law of peacebuilding appears somewhat partial. For example, while IHRL seems to loom large over the thoughts of these practitioners, other aspects such as the responsibility to rebuild or the issues around the laws of annexation seem to resonate less. A scholar/practitioner working on peace indicators across a range of countries points out that practitioners who do not have a legal background feel that the legal dimension of peacebuilding is dominated by human rights and human rights lawyers.[4] In this context, her experience has been that human rights lawyers tend to have limited knowledge of what peace involves and what are the requirements of peacebuilding. In particular, the granular work around community engagement, dialogue and reconciliation in peacebuilding are matters which lawyers seem less aware of. The issue of the pre-eminence of human rights law and related international criminal law (ICL) in the area of post-conflict peacebuilding is particularly noteworthy. As is the tendency for lawyers in these domains to focus exclusively on their subject matter, giving insufficient attention to the broader peacebuilding agenda.

Overall, international law seems to be acknowledged by CRP practitioners as one element (even an important one for some) of the conflict and post-conflict scenarios in which they operate. However, as alluded to earlier, it is only specific parts of international law that are so acknowledged. It is clear that ICL, especially in the context of dealing with mass atrocities, figures heavily in the literature on transitional justice and peacebuilding.[5]

In Bosnia-Herzegovina, ICL is of paramount importance and peace practitioners have either a reasonably good or considerable understanding of its key features. There is also concern about rule of law issues such as reform of the judiciary as well as corruption. In this latter case, while there is considerable attention to the issue, there is less clarity on the potential role of international law in their regard. Mostly, they are regarded as a matter in which the EU and Council of Europe play a major role. This has recently been more acute given Bosnia Herzegovina (BiH)'s EU candidate status. In the view of an official in the Office of the Ombudsperson of BiH, even lawyers in the country do not have an in-depth understanding of international law as law faculties within the universities do not devote sufficient attention to international law and it is only those lawyers who specialise in international law at postgraduate level who develop such knowledge.[6]

To take a different context, in Cyprus, the role of the international law of peacebuilding is regarded by some with suspicion given that for some the epithet post-conflict is unacceptable in the Cypriot case. They consider that the Cyprus conflict is still ongoing without a final resolution and therefore one cannot speak about an international law of peacebuilding prior to a peace agreement being signed.[7] Others, find this to be too narrow an approach and hold that peacebuilding initiatives between the communities in Cyprus have now been ongoing for decades and there should not be any artificial *a priori* bars to engaging with the international law of peacebuilding. The main substantive aspects of international law that have traction in Cyprus are the law prohibiting the use of force and IHRL (most specifically the role of the European Court of Human Rights in property disputes that emanated from the conflict). For instance, the Loizidou Case decided by the European Court of Human Rights in 1998 is familiar to peace practitioners and, possibly, to most Cypriots.

Within Northern Ireland, there is engagement with issues of international law such as self-determination, minority rights and IHRL generally.[8] For a period in the immediate post-conflict phase, arms decommissioning was an issue of great salience and to a more limited extent the reintegration of combatants (specifically members of paramilitary groups).[9] In more recent years, the attention of peacebuilding practitioners has shifted more towards what are termed legacy issues. However, while these are potentially part of the international law of peacebuilding as outlined in Chapters 1 and 2, they may not be viewed as such by all peace practitioners. The contrasts around this matter are evident in reactions to the Northern Ireland Troubles (Legacy and Reconciliation) Act 2023 enacted by the UK parliament. These frictions may also be attributable to the lack of clarity on what constitutes the international law of peacebuilding, coupled with the fact that it is yet to raise its profile outside the immediate circle of international law practitioners who have worked on its development.

It is also important to note that for peace practitioners, the existence of a peace agreement that governs the particular peacebuilding context may also impact the understanding of international law. A representative of the Office of the High Representative in BiH commented that for them the Dayton Peace Agreement is an important international law instrument and that it constitutes the international law of peacebuilding in BiH.[10] Peace practitioners in Northern Ireland likewise constantly utilise the frameworks provided by the Belfast Agreement with an eminent scholar stating that: "[p]ut bluntly, there is no acceptable alternative to the broad approach adopted in the Good Friday Agreement".[11] Even in Cyprus where no such agreement is in place, the Green Line Regulation adopted in the context of Cyprus' accession to the EU has, albeit to a more limited extent, played a similar role. Those engaged in shaping the international law of peacebuilding may want to examine in greater detail the limits of peace agreements, which will never be able to accommodate all potential contingencies and may very well avoid certain difficult areas of contention altogether in order to secure an agreement. While, self-evidently, these agreements play an essential role in the transition from violent conflict to sustainable peace, it is unlikely they will be able to cater for the totality of the requirement of peacebuilding in the medium-long term. Placing an excessive onus on such agreements may serve to both undermine them as well as detract attention from the larger international law peacebuilding framework that is being shaped.

It is equally worth considering that specific international (or regional) law instruments may have greater salience for peace practitioners than broader and more generally applicable international law normative frameworks. It is a matter of course that such context-specific instruments would have received much greater attention in the media and public arena than the more general international law instruments. For instance, the European Convention on Human Rights is specifically referenced in the Good Friday Agreement and has been a key factor in the Northern Ireland conflict and peace process.[12] The Statute of the Ad Hoc Tribunal for the Former Yugoslavia has the same status in terms of attention and awareness within BiH. This greater attention is also aided by the fact that such specific legal instruments, which are invariably codified, have a greater degree of clarity than the nascent law of international post-conflict peacebuilding.

The two issues of clarity and understanding/knowledge are clearly correlated. Until there is sufficient clarity as to what constitutes the international law of peacebuilding, raising its profile outside the confines of legal practitioners who are engaged with it will remain a tall order. As highlighted at the outset, generalisations ought to be treated with great caution. However, it seems clear that, to date, while peace scholars and practitioners in various contexts are aware of, and in some cases well-versed, in the general principles of international law and specific aspects of the international law of peacebuilding, they fail to see these parts as forming a distinct whole under the umbrella of *jus post bellum.* In summary, international law is given limited attention by the CRP community, while the international law of peacebuilding is either unknown or unused as a term or understood incompletely (specifically as IHRL and ICL).

Given the rather partial understanding and relatively limited knowledge of the international law of peacebuilding within the CRP community, it is problematic to assess attitudes towards the law of peacebuilding as a whole. To some extent, views on international law, in general, are coloured by personal experiences and biases towards the law more generally.

For instance, experiences of working with international organisations seem to translate to attitudes towards international law generally. A Bosnian scholar and peace practitioner commented that negative or challenging experiences of working with international organisations (particularly intergovernmental international organisations such as UN agencies, the EU or OSCE) may impact the perceptions around international law for peace practitioners working at the community level.[13] He commented that in some cases non-local practitioners from international organisations may not show sufficient regard to domestic laws and processes.

Other actors have positive attitudes towards international law based on the value-added which they consider that it brings to their work. For example, a member of the Balkan Investigative Network commented that they had fruitful cooperation with the International Criminal Tribunal for the Former Yugoslavia (ICTY) and that they use the ICTY judgments continuously in their daily work.[14] Specifically, she explained how the ICTY judgments were an important tool in their work to combat denial of crimes against humanity, etc. In one of their projects, they use ICTY testimonies and judgments to teach history to children and young people. Within this context, the perception in this organisation is that BiH needs external institutions and international law was beneficial to BiH as well as the broader region. In the same vein, they expressed the view that more effective international law norms are required for issues such as the right of return for 2.2 million persons who had to leave their homes during the war or the issue of missing persons.

The matter of the effectiveness of international law appears to be of particular concern. It has been suggested that working with peacebuilders on the ground one notes that there exists a certain frustration that international norms are frequently not applied. This leads to a general perception of international law as ineffectual, which may well decrease the appetite of practitioners and activists to engage with it.

Within Cyprus, the same dichotomy exists in relation to the perceptions and attitudes to international law. For some peace practitioners, international law is perceived as an ineffective tool in terms of resolving the conflict in the case of Cyprus. To this extent, the international law of peacebuilding obviously presents greater difficulties in contexts where the armed conflict is frozen rather than ended. It is worth noting that in the context of Cyprus, the official position of the Cypriot government is very much that the conflict is an ongoing one and cannot be considered terminated until Turkish troops withdraw from the island. Once again, the inability to enforce the international law norms relating to the prohibition of the use of force serves to limit the appeal of international law as a whole in the broader context of peacebuilding.

Finally, one notes that an unsurprising feature of reviewing the literature on conflict resolution and peace-building as well as in conversations with community-level CRP practitioners is how much the field is dominated by the specific local context of war and peace. The importance of the local context, the specific power structures and root causes of conflict are essential components of peacebuilding. Coleman in discussing the attitudes to power and conflict refers to the "importance of localized, situation-specific understanding"[15] in conflict resolution settings. Ramsbotham, Woodhouse and Miall equally emphasise the significance of a "nuanced understanding of local conditions".[16] The very relevance and meaning of international law depend to an extent –considerable in some cases – on the local conditions.

In BiH, the mention of international law in the context of the conflict is immediately met by references to ICL, as if by Pavlovian reflex. Issues relating to crimes against humanity and genocide remain front and centre of the dialogue between international law and the Bosnian conflict almost 30 years after the conflict formally ended. In Cyprus, the responses are chiefly about the use of force and property rights and specifically the right of return to properties owned prior to the armed conflict. In Northern Ireland, issues around self-determination have long dominated the discourse, while post-Peace Agreement, legacy issues have largely taken over most of the debate. In summary, the understanding of the international law of peacebuilding is at best partial and tied to contextual elements.

Inputs to the International Law of Peacebuilding From the CRP Community

Notwithstanding the limited engagement with the international law of peacebuilding by the CRP community, an exploration of some of the concepts and approaches developed by CRP scholars and practitioners may provide useful insights for the evolution of the international law of peacebuilding. I will summarise some of these concepts and approaches under three broad headings of (i) fundamental concepts, (ii) timing and prioritisation and (iii) actors and approaches.

The discipline of CRP has over the decades of its evolution developed a number of concepts that seek to explain the root causes of conflict, how to address these causes and how to attempt to transform relationships between conflicting parties in a sustainable manner. Basic notions such as the human needs theory of conflict, the concepts of structural and cultural violence, ideas on conflict transformation through repairing relations are examples of such fundamental concepts in CRP. It is suggested that legal scholars working on the development of the international law of peacebuilding need to engage more intimately with these concepts. In particular, the human needs theory of conflict, recognition of one's identity, the opportunity to participate in making meaningful public decisions and a distributive conception of justice are all identified as such. If we apply such a framework to the current status of the international law of peacebuilding, what insights might we obtain? Would we need to reconsider the IHRL regime, in any way, in light of participatory decision-making? Would the responsibility to reconstruct within the framework of R2P be impacted by the emphasis on distributive justice?

The consideration of the concepts of structural and cultural violence may likewise prompt a re-examination of the international law of peacebuilding in particular but also international law more broadly. The concept of cultural violence focuses on attitudes and beliefs that are prevalent in a community and that create violence. Structural violence emphasises an examination of societal structures (such as class, gender, nationality, etc.) that create systems that oppress some sectors of society and privilege others. The analysis of the role of structures in creating violence amongst groups – at the national or international level – has for some time now been a key concern of the CRP community. Rubenstein, for example, argues that conflicts having deep-rooted structural causes may not be peacefully resolved – let alone sustain the peace – by adopting traditional approaches since "methods appropriate to helping resolve other forms of conflict may not be sufficiently system-oriented to get at the roots of structural conflict".[17] Again, the consideration of and engagement with literature on cultural and structural violence and the conflicts that emerge therefrom would benefit the legal scholarship around the international law of peacebuilding. The displacement of cultural norms and societal structures that engender violence seems an admirable objective for the law of peacebuilding. What may be usefully incorporated into the normative processes from the insights, ideas and practice of CRP scholars and practitioners? At a higher level, international law as a whole, may be examined in light of structural conceptions of violence. To what extent is international law a normative framework that could be classified as a violent structure i.e. a structure that privileges some actors at the expense of others? Richard Falk offers this view of international law in the Cold War and post-Cold War periods, specifically in the context of conflict:

> In more recent times, international law in conflictual settings has generally served strategically as a propaganda tool for demonizing geopolitical and ideological enemies, as during the Cold War, as well as staking justice claims of moral superiority for our side in conflictual relations. The West and then "the free world" claimed to be the global disseminator of civilization, a guardian angel of manifest destiny, a trustworthy keeper of the peace, and the steadfast opponent of barbarism.[18]

If this is indeed the case – whether wholly or partially, how may we start thinking of transforming international law within conflict settings? CRP principles and approaches may be apposite tools to commence the process of re-imagining international law in conflictual settings.

Insofar as transformation is concerned, the concept of conflict transformation pioneered by Lederach and others is also noteworthy from a peacebuilding perspective. The concept of transformation emphasises that dealing with conflict and establishing a sustainable peace is not a moment in time but a process. Moreover, as with the structural conceptions mentioned above it conceives systemic change as being a primary aim of building peace. As emphasised by Notter and Diamond, systems (or structures) cannot be "resolved" but they can be transformed.[19] This thinking may be useful from a law of peacebuilding perspective because it helps us to think differently both around the time-frames that peacebuilding requires and also the priorities it should have. The emphasis is on process rather than on events. Thus, for example, elections in a post-conflict context are not a priority. Reconciliation processes, educational reforms, creating spaces for civil society and building grassroots constituencies for peaceful politics should be prioritised. International law practitioners involved in peacebuilding need to reflect on the assertion that for a successful transformation to peace, "the key lies in the relationship of the involved parties with all that the term implies at the psychological, spiritual, social, economic, political and military levels".[20] If this is so, then the international law of peacebuilding needs to focus on norms that enhance and nourish this relationship building. While the law cannot legislate for improving relations, it can prioritise (or – if appropriate – mandate) the establishment of structures and processes that nourish relational transformations.

The issue of prioritisation, phasing and time-frames has emerged as a critical one in peacebuilding and constitutes an important locus of intersection between the legal community engaged in this field and the broader CRP community. Ramsbotham et al. argue that peacebuilding should be seen as three interconnected (or nested) phases: intervention, stabilisation and normalisation with distinct but related priorities within each phase.[21]

It is axiomatic that, as demonstrated in the previous chapter, post-conflict settings present fragile, complex and disjointed realities where resources (financial and human) have to be allocated with care and deliberation. Decisions on what should be done and in what order, need to be taken. The international law of peacebuilding cannot and should not legislate on specific priorities, but it may give direction on the requirement of adopting fair and inclusive processes in decisions on allocation. Moreover, it may also direct that when such processes are being managed by external actors (whether international organisations or intervening states) decisions should be taken with decisive input from local actors at all levels. Citing Miall at al., Elham Atashi states that "[t]he literature on post-conflict transformation emphasizes that the sustainability of peace agreements requires top-down and bottom-up approaches or, in other words, involvement from the entire society".[22]

The international law of peacebuilding may also provide direction on which institutions and processes should be prioritised. In terms of priorities, a reading of certain analyses and experiences by CRP scholars and practitioners, apart from underlining the importance of general inclusivity, also highlights the need to (i) consider the dangers of "uneven peace processes" where those grassroots who are most impacted by the conflict are the least involved,[23] (ii) consider the view that substantial involvement by mid-range actors is particularly impactful in terms of peacebuilding[24] and (iii) consider the data gathered by CRP scholars showing that establishing local government processes in post-conflict situations reduces the chances of relapse into violence.[25]

Perhaps the area of the international law of peacebuilding that may most usefully intersect with the CRP conceptions of priorities, phasing and timeframes is that of ICL and the matter of dealing with perpetrators of mass atrocities. As mentioned in previous chapters, this branch of international law has caused significant divergences, most often summarised as the "peace v justice" dichotomy. Some CRP scholars and practitioners have identified the adoption of long timeframes as indispensable to peacebuilding. Scholars such as Lederach urges a rethink of timeframes when it comes to peacebuilding. What may these approaches mean for international law? Should it rethink its emphasis on no amnesties or consider whether, within the complexities inherent post-conflict situations, a slower pace to international criminal justice may be more conducive to sustainable peace? Or even that in the context of priorities and phasing, dealing with mass atrocities should be a middle to long-term objective rather than an immediate priority?

For those involved in conflict resolution and peacebuilding who are from the IHRL tradition (as I do), such questions may sound uncomfortable. They may reek of pragmatism or worse. However, in the quest to build sustainable peace, the focus should remain firmly on reconciliating conflicting parties, repairing broken relations and reforming oppressive systems and cultures. Advocates of ICL and IHRL should accept that in some contexts and some peacebuilding phases, they may not be the most effective means to the peacebuilding objective. This should not be anathema to the legal community where balancing rights and interests is a daily process. In fact, the need to balance the requirements of punitive justice with the broader requirements of reconciliation has been acknowledged by judicial bodies such as the South African Constitutional Court. In the case of *Azanian People's Organization v President of the Republic of South Africa*, the court rejected a claim that the family of Steve Biko had a right to the prosecution of his killer, even though an amnesty had been granted to the killer by South Africa's Truth and Reconciliation Commission. The court held that South Africa's needs for reconciliation had to be given priority over the family's right to see justice done.[26]

As mentioned earlier in this section, CRP scholars have also sought to identify the actors whose engagement in peacebuilding seems to engender the greatest degree of sustainability. The need for local ownership of the peacebuilding venture is a generally accepted principle advocated by CRP scholars and practitioners as is inclusivity and the need for a "whole of society" endeavour.[27] Ramsbotham et al. articulate the received wisdom in this context as follows:

> ...genuine peacebuilding means an abandonment of uniform and bureaucratically imposed structures, a far greater sensitivity and nuanced understanding of local conditions and a readiness to encompass the variety of voices, often conflicting, that must participate if there is to be inclusive "collective" reasoning about the peace building project.[28]

Others have indicated that focusing on what are described as mid-range actors (such as local community leaders who are connected both to the elites and the grassroots) is an efficient *modus operandi* in the early to mid-term, in order to establish what Lederach terms a peace infrastructure, within which efforts towards positive peace can evolve.[29] The relevance of grassroots engagement with peacebuilding has also been a matter of attention in CRP research.[30] In particular, it has been suggested that attention should be drawn to directly impacted conflict zones and "[a]reas where violence and deprivation have been consistent throughout the conflict should be given priority. This strategy should direct tangible resources that will create opportunities among the people who have been impacted most by the conflict".[31] The essential point is that if the (necessary) elite-level peacemaking process is not accompanied by parallel processes within the community at all levels the possibilities of successful transformation towards positive peace diminish. Those who are least engaged in the transformation and who benefit least from it are less likely to support it and more likely to turn into spoilers (especially if a section of the elite decides to withdraw or undermine the process). Tangible benefits arriving early in such conflict areas, in terms of access to decision-making, educational and economic opportunities, as well as the establishment of community-based initiatives (political, social, cultural, etc.), can help sustain the peacebuilding project.

All of these insights, present opportunities for reflection within the ambit of the international law of peacebuilding.[32] The indication of priority areas and actors is perhaps not a matter that can be given mandatory normative force, given the desirability of avoiding rigid normative forms in peacebuilding whenever possible. However, priority indicators may well form part of guidelines that can gradually evolve into what, in a slightly different context, Christopher Mitchell terms "En-Acted Constraint",[33] i.e., well-known and widely – but not universally – accepted modes of conduct. What may, and in my view should, be mandated by the international law of peacebuilding are the principles of localism (in its simplest form this means that definitive as opposed to interim decisions are taken by local actors) and "whole of society" approaches, where the elites are not allowed to dominate the process of achieving positive peace.

In terms of approaches to peacebuilding one, that has attracted attention from both the legal and CRP communities is the role of democratisation. Democratisation – in the form of the market economy-based liberal democracy – has featured as an element of peacebuilding since the late 1980s. As Lyons has remarked, "[t]he liberal internationalist paradigm posits that peace, both between and within states, is based on market democracy and that constructing democratic political structures is key to sustainable peace".[34] The reference to democratic political structures has often been translated into elections at all costs, even where the conditions for such electoral contests were absent. The experiences in Afghanistan, Iraq and Libya are instructive in this regard. This approach has been subjected to criticism from CRP scholars and practitioners but the reality shows that elections have remained high on the agenda of the UN as part of the peacebuilding process. In a 2010 UN document "support to political processes, including electoral processes" was identified as an early need that should be prioritised in the first 24 months after the cessation of hostilities.

Another perspective that has emerged regarding the approach to democratisation in the aftermath of conflict is that of widening the prevailing understanding of democratic models. That the Western model of majoritarian democracy is not a panacea is evident (and is becoming evident in Western democracies themselves). The need to widen understanding of what democratic models may look like and the importance of building on local traditions and customary practices is a relevant consideration. Bartoli et al. have commented on how in Mozambique – which until the 2017 Islamist insurgency had witnessed a successful peace process – the blending of local customs with Western ideas on democracy had a fair degree of success.[35] Lederach also advocates the need to build on local expertise and understandings in this sphere when he emphasises the "need to build on the cultural resources for peace and conflict resolution present within the setting".[36]

One hopes that the experiences of Afghanistan and Libya, amongst others, will provide salutary lessons on the rush to elections. The phenomenon of elections without democracy has not withstood the test of time. Lyons suggests that in post-conflict settings there are limited alternatives to electoral processes and that what needs to be considered are processes that demilitarise politics before the electoral competition. He argues that where elections have been a successful component of peacebuilding (South Africa, Mozambique, Nicaragua and El Salvador are given as examples) "key processes to 'demilitarize politics' were in place before the vote".[37] It is unlikely that the international law of peacebuilding will depart from its consensus on matters such as democratisation, rule of law and human rights which are endorsed by the current UN principles on peacebuilding. However, international law may reconsider the prioritisation of electoral competitions and especially distinguish between democratic processes and elections. The demilitarisation of politics, the decommissioning of weapons, the promotion of consultative fora and other dialogic spaces as well as spaces for civil society activities may all be requisite precursors to electoral politics. The international law of peacebuilding should clarify that these processes are at the core of democratisation and that democratic processes may be informed by local (non-Western) experiences and practices.

Even where democratic processes take root and elections are held in more-or-less stable environments, the possibility of spoilers attempting to derail the peacebuilding agenda is always present. This is a matter of concern in any peace process. The possibility of a group or sub-group within a peace process deciding whether to officially or surreptitiously spoil the process is a question which has been examined by the CRP community both with respect to peace negotiations and the post-agreement peacebuilding phase. Mac Ginty, for instance, has called for the need to accept that peace processes will be contested and that actors and institutions should not be tied to the notion of a perfect peace. Calling for a high threshold of tolerance for spoiling behaviour, he argues that

> it is crucial that those involved in a peace process (at both the elite and grassroots levels) internalize the notion of a contested peace and use it when rationalizing spoiling behaviour.[38]

Within this perspective, the international law of peacebuilding should consider what mechanisms may be incorporated that allow for an internalisation of what Mac Ginty terms "contested peace". The importance of having resilient peacebuilding processes is self-evident. Scholars and practitioners of CRP may surely contribute towards crafting guidelines that present avenues for increasing the resilience of peace processes, even by lowering expectations as to what the peacebuilding journey may achieve in the short to medium term.

One group of actors that have the potential to act as spoilers are ex-combatants both because of their experience of violence and access to weapons. Thus, considerable attention has been paid to the reintegration of former combatants into civilian life. The CRP community has examined this aspect of post-conflict practice in some detail. As mentioned in Chapter 2, international law has also taken some tentative steps in this regard through the UN.

Peace education is another approach to peacebuilding which merits attention. In fact, I suggest it is a promising area for collaborative work between international law scholars and practitioners and CRP scholars and practitioners. In particular, international human rights lawyers within CRP are involved with integrating human rights laws, practices and processes in post-conflict peacebuilding. In fact, human rights lawyers were for a time seen as polemical presences in CRP contexts with their insistence on documenting and condemning human rights violations in conflict settings.[39]

The view of the relationship between rights and CRP has evolved since then[40] although the matter of responding to mass violations of human rights remains problematic and contentious. Nevertheless, a more holistic approach to examining the relationship between human rights and CRP has emerged. In such a context, the emphasis on education deserves sustained attention. IHRL provides – in various treaties[41] – for a the right to education. The Universal Declaration of Human Rights lists the right to education as one of the original human rights. Article 26 of the Declaration establishes the right to education in two parts. In the first part, the article sets out the general right to education for everyone (including the provision of free education). However, the second component of article 26 sets out the "kind" of education we all have a right to:

> Education shall be directed to the full development of the human personality and to the strengthening of respect for human rights and fundamental freedoms. It shall promote understanding, tolerance and friendship among all nations, racial or religious groups, and shall further the activities of the United Nations for the maintenance of peace.

This provision and the equivalent ones in international human rights treaties explicate the qualitative nature of the right to education in three main directions: (i) the development of the human personality in all its dimensions, (ii) an education for human rights with all that this implies in terms of building respect for the human rights of all other persons and (iii) an education that promotes understanding, tolerance, friendship and peace. These three dimensions of the right to education may all be conducive to productive debates amongst legal and CRP scholars and practitioners on how they may be best interpreted and applied within post-conflict peacebuilding contexts. Ramsbotham et al argue that "the development of peace education [is] a central component of peacebuilding" and that it

> provides an opportunity both to embed the core values of conflict resolution around non-violence and emancipation and to define a transformative cosmopolitan model which seeks to apply these values in peacebuilding.[42]

Thus, rather than focus on dogmatic and sterile debates as to whether IHRL lawyers are an obstacle to conflict resolution in the limited context of responding to mass human rights violations, the attention should shift to the potential for peacebuilding offered by the right to education within IHRL. Human rights education and peace education both of which are clear components of the right to education share a number of characteristics.

Primarily, they are both part of the values-based education that is so essential in post-conflict peacebuilding.

This type of education which aims at changing behaviour rather than increasing knowledge seems to align with the CRP focus on relational issues such as reconciliation. UNESCO has for many years focused on this type of education. It is noteworthy that in 2023 at the 42nd session of its General Conference, it adopted a revised Recommendation on Education for Peace, Human Rights and Sustainable Development. The process that led to the adoption of the revised Recommendation included strong elements of multi-stakeholder involvement which are interesting in the context of Chapter 5. The document is intended as a "standard-setting instrument that lays out how education should be used to bring about lasting peace and foster human development through 14 guiding principles".[43] The approach of adopting guidelines rather than more binding forms reflects the already cited preference for flexible approaches which are more conducive to adoption and adaption in post-conflict settings.

Given that the right to education, as codified in international law, has a significant role within peacebuilding, it is a promising area where expertise from both the legal and CRP communities may usefully collaborate. Issues around balancing the rights of parents to choose educational institutions for their children with the need for an education that promotes diversity, tolerance and understanding may be especially fraught in post-conflict societies. In such an aspect, the interaction of CRP practitioners and human rights lawyers may be especially fruitful in devising appropriate principles and guidelines.

The promotion and protection of women's rights within international human rights frameworks is another area which may be conducive to positive and sustained interaction between the international law community as well as CRP practitioners and scholars. IHRL has, since the 1960s at least, focused significantly on recognising women's rights as an essential component of the global human rights agenda.[44] The increasing focus on women's rights in international law led to the mainstreaming of the promotion of women's rights and their equal participation in public life, both within the UN and also within regional organizations. In fact, building on the international human rights obligations of all UN member states, the Fourth World Conference on Women held in Beijing in 1995 gender mainstreaming was endorsed as a strategic approach for achieving gender equality commitments.[45] In the context of peacebuilding, it is also notable that the Conference was subtitled "Action for Equality Development and Peace".

The impact of the rise of women's rights has also been evident in the field of peacebuilding, with the UN Security Council adopting resolution 1325 in October 2000. The resolution called for increased "representation of women at all decision-making levels in national, regional and international institutions and mechanisms for the prevention, management, and resolution of conflict". Since then, the issue of the role of women in peacebuilding has expanded within CRP. The academic literature on the subject has also increased. One recent study suggests that women in peacebuilding may be a factor for successful transitions to positive peace:

> The empirical analysis presented in this study strongly attests to the significant role that women can play in post-conflict reconstruction. As the empirical analysis based on disaggregated data from the UN peacebuilding missions in Liberia and Sierra Leone suggests, programs like DDR and community projects elicit more cooperation by the local populations towards the presence and the role of the UN. Thus, women's organizations, especially in countries like Liberia with a long history of women's activism, can be involved both in the planning and implementation phases of a project to increase the probability of success.[46]

It thus seems clear that the spaces occupied by women's rights in international law and that which focuses on the role of women in peacebuilding not only overlap but may constitute common ground upon which the IHRL community and the CRP community may have a dynamic and productive engagement.

This chapter concludes with a brief investigation of how the intersection between international law norms and peacebuilding are viewed in the context of a specific peacebuilding process, i.e., that of BiH. This exercise will provide a snapshot of how the preceding discussion reflects itself (if at all) on the ground in a particular location.

A Postscript on International Law and Peacebuilding: A Snapshot From Bosnia Herzegovina

BiH presents a pertinent case study to examine the complex relationships between international law and the peacebuilding community. It has been navigating the aftermath of violent conflict for almost 30 years. This span of time provides a degree of *long durée* that allows for a degree of perspective on the intersections between peacebuilders and international law in the context of a state which, like numerous others, has been dealing with two concurrent transitions. A transition from an authoritarian to a democratic system and the transition we are particularly focusing on from conflict to peace. In such a context, the prioritization between peacebuilding and democratisation, discussed above, becomes an additional and important dimension to the peacebuilding community. In this section, we delve into the attitudes towards international law within the context of peacebuilding in BiH, exploring perspectives on its roles, challenges and implications.

As evidenced in the preceding chapters, the transition from conflict to peace involves multifaceted processes, including infrastructural development, institutional restructuring and post-conflict reconciliation. One of the dilemmas that arise in a situation such as BiH is determining the primacy between peacebuilding and democratic transition. While both are interconnected, and democratisation is included as an element of peacebuilding (see above) establishing clear priorities is a relevant consideration.

The easy answer is that both transitions are equally important and should be given equal attention and space. However, the reality is that in situations such as BiH resources are always limited in terms of both human and financial terms. The question thus emerges: Should the focus be on consolidating peace or advancing democratic governance? Moreover, who holds the authority to decide on these priorities amidst divergent interests and stakeholders? In the context of BiH, as in others, the peacebuilding community asks the question as to who is legitimised in making these decisions. Should international law provide guidelines as to how decisions on national/community priorities should be taken?

As pointed out by a Bosnian academic and peace practitioner, these are not simply theoretical or academic questions:

> BiH is not just a post-conflict society but also a post-authoritarian one. There was no tradition of democratic processes that could be built upon. Thus. as in other similar situations, we are combining two processes: a democratic transition and a post-conflict peacebuilding process. I am not suggesting these are entirely separate agendas as much as that they engage different priorities. International organisations also have their own priorities and the different nationalities represented in these organisations may also have different approaches which complicates matters. Therefore, there is a difficulty in ensuring consistent processes in building peace.[47]

This view also clearly distinguishes the transition to positive peace from the transition to democracy. One may suggest that in cases where national stakeholders and international institutions (whether it is the UN, EU, Organization for Security and Cooperation in Europe (OSCE) or others) may have different priorities, an international legal framework that coordinates such differentiated positions would assist in having consistent peacebuilding processes. A set of guidelines that provides direction on how to prioritise the multifaceted agendas in peacebuilding is lacking. The domestic and international peacebuilding communities would play a pivotal role in developing such guidelines. The preceding discussion shows that CRP scholars and practitioners would direct the decision-making primarily towards the local community.

A key factor that influences attitudes to international law within any peacebuilding context is knowledge of international law amongst the peacebuilding community. It is clear that knowledge of the international law of peacebuilding is not widely reflected within CRP academic literature. In terms of understanding international law in BiH, particularly as it concerns peacebuilding, this has largely been dominated by a focus on ICL and IHRL. Those involved in post-conflict peacebuilding seem at least aware of ICL and IHRL. A Bosnian civil society organisation that focuses on media in peacebuilding argued that the role of ICL and the Ad Hoc Tribunal in particular was an aspect that permeated through most of their work. However, when pressed further on what other aspects of international law they considered important for peacebuilding, the responses were less forthcoming.

This twin focus on ICL and IHRL, while understandable given the prevailing circumstances in BiH, served to underscore a rather limited perspective of international law within the country, including amongst the peacebuilding community. Consequently, the multifarious aspects of the international law of peacebuilding highlighted in the first two chapters are not engaged with to any great extent within BiH. A leading member of the Office of the Ombudsman in BiH expressed the view that not only was knowledge of international law limited within the peacebuilding community in BiH but also within the legal community as well. It was pointed out that legal education in the country was not providing sufficient emphasis on international law.[48] As cited earlier, an official within the Office of the High Representative in Sarajevo considered the Dayton Agreement as their (only) lodestar.

These comments underscore the need for a better and more rounded understanding of international law in peacebuilding contexts. While ICL and IHRL are considered essential components of the international law of post-conflict peacebuilding, an undue focus on these issues provides only a partial understanding of the role and potential of international law in peacebuilding.

In the case of BiH, perceptions of international law in the context of peacebuilding are also coloured by the association of international legal frameworks with bureaucratic entities such as the European EU and the UN, which are perceived as rigid and distant from local realities.[49] For instance, the fact that the presence of these organisations is largely limited to cities and larger towns with smaller towns and rural areas being excluded was highlighted as a weakness in terms of inclusivity.[50] This is an interesting insight that is worthy of further investigation and coincides with the concern around elites which permeates the CRP literature. The extent to which international law is seen as an extraneous and elitist force, and its association with bureaucratic organisations or, in some cases, colonial powers, is a matter of concern in all cases, but particularly in post-conflict settings.

Furthermore, the technical nature of international law, particularly evident to the youth, contributes to disengagement and apathy towards its principles. The failure of international legal mechanisms to adequately integrate and recognise the local legal culture and principles exacerbates this disconnect. The disparity between domestic laws and international legal standards, exemplified by the discrepancy in sentencing between national and international courts, raises questions about the efficacy and legitimacy of international interventions. It was suggested that legal experts whether in media settings or official or civil society meetings tend to utilise legal discourse which is not very conducive to engagement by those from around the legal community (a point which may resonate from Chapter 3). In the words of a civil society peacebuilding practitioner of long-standing: "it either puts people off or switches them off".[51]

At the same time, the same practitioner acknowledged that lawyers in BiH are perceived to possess certain advantages in navigating the intricacies of international legal frameworks, particularly concerning human rights and criminal law. They are also deemed to have a capacity in terms of drafting which is useful in situations which require such writing skills. At the same time, the emphasis on technical skill and legalistic processes may obscure the broader socio-political dimensions of conflict resolution and reconciliation, perpetuating a cycle of legalistic approaches divorced from local realities.

Moreover, the fact that reconciliation issues are underexplored in international law and any normative developments in this context are largely unknown, may also hamper the positioning of international law of peacebuilding as an integral part of peacebuilding efforts, rather than just as a specific aspect of transitional justice. Multiple individuals involved in the peacebuilding process in BiH were unable to point out any other aspects of international law with which they had familiarity or which they considered could be usefully addressed by international law.

While NGOs have endeavoured to fill this void, the relegation of reconciliation to the periphery of legal frameworks impedes the deeper and broader engagement between the legal community and the CRP community. The narrow focus on ICL and IHRL further exacerbates this gap, neglecting critical areas such as environmental law that are integral to sustainable peace and development.

The attitude towards international law in the context of peacebuilding in BiH reflects a complex interplay of perspectives, challenges and aspirations. While international legal frameworks provide essential mechanisms for accountability and justice, their limitations in addressing reconciliation and holistic peacebuilding efforts underscore the need for a paradigm shift. To some extent, the snapshot of BiH underscores some of the concerns expressed in this as well as in the preceding chapters. The need to bridge the gap between legal formalism and pragmatic peacebuilding is a real one. The Bosnian snapshot indicates that such bridging requires a concerted effort to integrate local perspectives, prioritise reconciliation and redefine the role (and language) of legal practitioners in facilitating meaningful and sustainable peace.

Conclusion

This chapter has sought to explore the extent to which the international law of peacebuilding is "on the radar" of the CRP community and how the latter community views the role of international law of peacebuilding. It has also engaged in a preliminary attempt at identifying some of the CRP principles and approaches which may assist in informing and shaping the development of the international law of peacebuilding. It has done so more as interrogation than answer. Each of the elements that go towards building the international law of peacebuilding may be informed and improved by a structured and sustained engagement with the principles and processes developed by the CRP community. Such a structured and sustained deserves a full study on its own.

Nonetheless, even the interrogatory approach adopted in this chapter reveals certain trends. Firstly, the international law of peacebuilding as described in Chapters 1 and 2 remains predominantly a concern of the legal community. It does not feature, in any meaningful way, as a term nor as a rounded concept in the mainstream CRP literature (including in the main textbooks and handbooks used to form the CRP community of the future). International law in the context of peacebuilding is seen as an expression of ICL (generally, in the framework of transitional justice) and of IHRL (generally, as part of peace agreements). These may be good starting points to develop the engagement between the legal and CRP communities suggested above. However, they are in themselves, insufficient. For the evolution of a comprehensive and coherent international law of post-conflict peacebuilding, a far greater awareness of its components is required amongst the CRP community. This is a *sine qua non* for engagement.

Apart from awareness, the absence of a clear, cohesive framework for the international law of peacebuilding (a matter referred to in Chapters 1 and 2) leaves practitioners grappling with disparate legal principles and processes. Moreover, the gap between legal theory and practical application poses obstacles to effective implementation on the ground. While certain legal instruments, such as IHRL and humanitarian law, receive recognition and utilization, broader frameworks of peacebuilding law remain elusive to many practitioners.

In terms of specific issues that arise from CRP theory and practice, the issues of inclusivity and localism; the focus on structures and systems; and the fundamental role of prioritisation and timing all emerge as critical aspects that the international law of peacebuilding needs to be influenced by and internalise. The exact shape and form of the relationship between international law and the CRP principles and processes require further practical examination through an increased interaction between the legal scholar-practitioners involved in the creation of international law of peacebuilding and the CRP community of scholar-practitioners.

Bridging the gap between legal theory and grassroots practice requires concerted efforts to enhance understanding, promote interdisciplinary dialogue and foster meaningful engagement across diverse stakeholder groups. By acknowledging the contextual nuances and challenges inherent in post-conflict settings, stakeholders can work towards developing a more coherent and responsive legal framework that addresses the multifaceted dynamics of peacebuilding. The ways in which, and places where, this multistakeholder engagement can take place is the subject of the next chapter.

Notes

1 Interview with Professor Pamina Firchow, online discussion with author, 21 August 2023.
2 I have failed to locate references to the literature on the international law of peacebuilding (reviewed in Chapter 1) in the literature on conflict resolution and peacebuilding which I consulted.
3 Falk, L. R. (2022). International Law. In *Encyclopedia of Violence, Peace, & Conflict* (3rd edition, volume 1), ed. Kurtz, L. Cambridge: Academic Press: 106–114.
4 Interview with Professor Pamina Firchow.
5 There is substantive literature on dealing with mass atrocities both in terms of transitional justice as well as international criminal justice perspectives. Some examples include Minow, M. (1999). *Between Vengeance and Forgiveness: Facing History After Genocide and Mass Violence*. Boston: Beacon Press; Hinton, A. L. (2011). T*ransitional Justice: Global Mechanisms and Local Realities After Genocide and Mass Violence*. New Brunswick: Rutgers University Press; Roberti di Sarsina, J. (2019). *Transitional Justice and a State's Response to Mass Atrocity*. Berlin: Springer; Lawther, C. and Moffett, L. (2023). *Research Handbook on Transitional Justice*. Cheltenham: Edward Elgar Publishing.
6 Interview with an official within the Office of the Ombudsperson, in discussion with the author, Sarajevo, Bosnia Herzegovina, 7 March 2023.
7 Interview with an official with the Ministry of Foreign Affairs of the Republic of Cyprus, in discussion with the author, Nicosia, Cyprus, 2 October 2022.
8 See inter alia Grech, *Human Rights and the Northern Ireland Conflict.*
9 For an examination of the salient issues in the immediate aftermath of Good Friday Agreement see inter alia Tonge, J. (2002). *Northern Ireland: Conflict and Change*, 2nd edition. New York: Routledge.
10 Interview with an official of the Office of the High Representative for Bosnia Herzegovina, online discussion with the author, 17 March 2023.
11 McCrudden, C. (2018). Twenty Years on from the Good Friday Agreement. The British Academy Blog. https://www.thebritishacademy.ac.uk/blog/twenty-years-good-friday-agreement/
12 For a full analysis of the ECHR and the conflict see Dickson, B. (2012). *The European Convention on Human Rights and the Conflict in Northern Ireland.* Oxford: Oxford University Press.
13 Interview with a professor from the University of Sarajevo, in discussion with the author, Sarajevo, Bosnia and Herzegovina, 8 March 2023.
14 Interview with representatives of the Balkan Investigative Network, in discussion with the author, Sarajevo, Bosnia and Herzegovina, 8 March 2023.
15 Deutsch M., Coleman P., Marcus E. (eds). (2014). *The Handbook of Conflict Resolution: Theory and Practice*, 3rd edition. Josey-Bass
16 Ramsbotham, Woodhouse and Miall. *Contemporary Conflict Resolution.* Cambridge.
17 Rubenstein, R. E. (2017). *Resolving Structural Conflicts.* Oxon: Routledge: 3.
18 Falk, R. International Law. In *Encyclopedia of Violence, Peace, & Conflict*, ed. Kurtz, L.: 106.
19 Nitter, J. and Diamond, L. (1996). Building Peace and Transforming Conflict: Multi-Track Diplomacy in Practice. The Institute for Multi-Track Diplomacy: Occasional Paper Number 7.

20 Lederach, J. P. *Building Peace*:75.
21 Ramsbotham, Woodhouse and Miall. *Contemporary Conflict Resolution:* 249–261.
22 Atashi, E. (2009). Challenges to Conflict Transformation from the Streets. In *Conflict Transformation and Peacebuilding*, ed. Dayton, B. W. and Kriesberg, L., 45. London: Routledge.
23 Atashi in *Conflict Transformation and Peacebuilding,* Dayton and Kriesberg: 45.
24 Lederach, *Building Peace*.
25 Dayton and Kriesberg: 3.
26 *Azanian People's Organization (AZAPO) v President of the Republic of South Africa*, 25 July 1996, CCT17/96, ZACC 16.
27 See, for example, Donais, T. (2012). *Peacebuilding and Local Ownership: Post-Conflict Consensus-Building*. Oxon: Routledge and Ramsbotham, Woodhouse and Miall. *Contemporary Conflict Resolution.*
28 Ramsbotham, Woodhouse and Miall. *Contemporary Conflict Resolution:* 266.
29 Lederach, *Building Peace*: 60.
30 For interesting insights on grassroots-driven peace initiatives see Mitchell, C. R. and Hancock, L. E. (2012). *Local Peacebuilding and National Peace: Interaction between Grassroots and Elite Processes*. New York: Bloomsbury Publishing.
31 Atashi in *Conflict Transformation and Peacebuilding,* Dayton and Kriesberg: 57.
32 United Nations. (2010). *UN Peacebuilding: An Orientation*: 12.
33 Mitchell, C. (2014). *The Nature of Intractable Conflict: Resolution in the Twenty-First Century*. London: Palgrave Macmillan: 184.
34 Lyons, T. Peacebuilding, Democratization, and Transforming the Institutions of War. In *Conflict Transformation and Peacebuilding*, eds Dayton, B. W. and Kriesberg, L.: 91.
35 Bartoli, A., Civico, A. and Gianturco, L. Mozambique-Renamo. In *Conflict Transformation and Peacebuilding*, eds Dayton, B. W. and Kriesberg, L.: 150–151.
36 Lederach, *Building Peace*: 95.
37 Lyons, T. Peacebuilding, Democratization, and Transforming the Institutions of War. In *Conflict Transformation and Peacebuilding*, eds Dayton, B. W. and Kriesberg, L.: 91.
38 Mac Ginty, R. (2006). Northern Ireland: A Peace Process Thwarted by Accidental Spoiling. In *Challenges to Peacebuilding: Managing Spoilers During Conflict Resolution*, eds Newman, E. and Richmond, O. Tokyo: UNU Press: 170
39 See, for example, Anonymous. (1996). Human Rights and Conflict. *Human Rights Quarterly* 18 (2): 249–258.
40 See, for example, Grech, O. *Human Rights and the Conflict Cycle*.
41 *International Covenant on Economic, Social and Cultural Rights*, 16 December 1966, Article 13 (entered into force 3 January 1976) and *United Nations Convention of the Rights of the Child.*
42 Ramsbotham, Woodhoose and Miall. *Contemporary Conflict Resolution*: 279.
43 See UNESCO. (2023). What You Need to Know About UNESCO's Recommendation on Education for Peace, Human Rights and Sustainable Development. https://www.unesco.org/en/articles/what-you-need-know-about-unescos-recommendation-education-peace-human-rights-and-sustainable (accessed May 28, 2024).
44 In 1967, United Nations Member States adopted the Declaration on the Elimination of Discrimination against Women which was followed by the Convention on the Elimination of All Forms of Discrimination against Women that was adopted by the General Assembly in 1979. Both are important milestones in this respect as is the Beijing Declaration and Programme of Action adopted at the Fourth World Conference on Women held in Beijing in September 1995.
45 UN. (1995). Report of the Fourth World Conference on Women: 119. https://www.un.org/womenwatch/daw/beijing/pdf/Beijing%20full%20report%20E.pdf (accessed May 28, 2024)

46 Gizelis, T. I. (2011). A Country of Their Own. Women and Peacebuilding. *Conflict Management and Peace Science* 28 (5): 522–542.
47 Interview with Professor Midhat Izmirlija from the University of Sarajevo, in discussion with the author, Sarajevo, Bosnia and Herzegovina, 8 March 2023.
48 Interview with an official Office of the Ombudsperson, Sarajevo, Bosnia Herzegovina, in discussion with the author, Sarajevo, Bosnia and Herzegovina, 8 March 2023.
49 Interview with Professor Midhat Izmirlija from the University of Sarajevo, in discussion with the author, Sarajevo, Bosnia and Herzegovina, 8 March 2023.
50 Interview with Professor Midhat Izmirlija from the University of Sarajevo and Interview with a representative of the Network for Building Peace, Sarajevo, Bosnia and Herzegovina, 7 March 2023.
51 Interview with a representative of the Network for Building Peace, Sarajevo, Bosnia and Herzegovina, 7 March 2023.

5 Locating Sites for a Multistakeholder Approach

Introduction

The preceding chapter ended with a call for the adoption of a multistakeholder approach to the development of the international law of post-conflict peacebuilding. In this chapter, the extent to which this has been happening so far will be gauged and possibilities for an intensification of this approach will be presented.

For such an approach to gain traction and become a primary locus of development of international law in the field of peacebuilding a number of factors must coalesce. Firstly, there must be a willingness on the part of the CRP community and the legal community to cooperate, as equals, in such ventures. It is difficult to determine accurately the exact degree of interest from the CRP community to engage more with the international law of peacebuilding as a branch of international law. It is instructive that a number of CRP scholars who were approached for an interview prefaced their comments with the proviso that they did not deal with legal issues or that they were not sure whether they could contribute or even declined to be interviewed as they felt their work was not concerned with legal matters. My response was that it was precisely because they were not lawyers that I valued their views and assuaged some, but not others. This hesitancy demonstrates that at least a few members of the community have the perception that international law is either too specialistic or irrelevant to them.

Conversely, in specific contexts there is considerable interest with engaging more and more deeply with already well-established components of this branch, like international human rights law and international criminal law. Indeed, in the context of Bosnia Herzegovina, several actors expressed disappointment that international legal institutions (primarily the International Criminal Tribunal for Yugoslavia; ICTY) did not, early on, engage sufficiently with the community-level peacebuilding organisations.[1]

Irrespective of the precise degree of interest by the CRP community in international law, it is clear that international law requires more engagement with this community. A major risk in the evolution of an international law

DOI: 10.4324/9781003462248-5

of post-conflict peacebuilding is that this initiative is viewed as just another branch of international law imposed on the peacebuilding sector. As such, it may be viewed as having little practical value in meeting the daily challenges faced by conflict resolution and peace practitioners. All the international law practitioners I spoke to concurred on the need to engage substantially with the CRP community as they were indispensable partners in evolving international law. One scholar of international law suggested that the field needed many more social psychologists and fewer lawyers.[2]

Before proceeding to discuss existing initiatives that sought to bring a multistakeholder approach to the international law of peacebuilding, it is worth considering the notion of multistakeholder decision-making (or in the present case decision-shaping). The fundamental idea is based on the values of inclusion, shared expertise (and information) and mutual recognition. In form, it consists of equal participation in decision-making/shaping processes of those individuals and entities who are concerned by the outcome(s) of those particular decision-making/shaping processes. Those individuals and entities who are concerned as to the outcome(s) are the stakeholders.

The idea of multistakeholder approaches within the framework of international relations and international law may be traced back to the United Nations Conference on Environment and Development held in Rio de Janeiro in June 1992. As Dodds points out, the non-binding but influential Agenda 21 that was agreed to at the Rio Summit was "the first UN document to recognise the roles and responsibilities of nine stakeholder groups".[3] By 1998, the UN Secretary-General was publicly acknowledging the changing nature of UN decision-making processes by stating that:

> The United Nations once dealt only with governments. By now we know that peace and prosperity cannot be achieved without partnerships involving governments, international organizations, the business community and civil society.[4]

Since then, the concept of multistakeholder approaches in international decision-making/shaping has taken root. One early example related to efforts to create a forum for global governance of the internet. With the rise of the internet in the late 1990s and early 2000s, the need to create international governance structures for the internet became an increasingly pressing concern. In dealing with this matter, the UN adopted a multistakeholder approach with the World Summit on Information Society held in 2003 and 2005 in Geneva and Tunis. These summits had considerable participation from civil society, including academic and technical experts in internet governance.

One outcome was the establishment of the Working Group on Internet Governance (WGIG), set up by the Secretary-General of the United Nations in accordance with the mandate given to him during the first phase of the Summit. The WGIG comprised 40 members from Governments, private sector and civil society, who all participated on an equal footing and in their personal capacity. This, in turn, led to the establishment of the Internet Governance Forum in 2005 again based on the principle of multistakeholder participation. The Forum will be holding its 19th annual meeting in Riyadh in December 2024 with the title "Building our Multistakeholder Digital Future". The longevity of the process as well as the continuing insistence on the multi-stakeholder dimension, illustrate the pertinence of creating sites where issues of global concern (and peacebuilding is evidently one such issue) may be the subject of informed discussion from a variety of perspectives with a view to improving the global governance of such issues.

In this chapter, the existence of such sites in the context of the international law of peacebuilding will be explored and other sites where multistakeholder decision-shaping may be attempted will be proposed.

Existing Multistakeholder Initiatives

The need to adopt a multistakeholder approach in the progressive development of international law norms related to post-conflict peacebuilding has already been recognised in some contexts. An example worth considering is the process that led to the adoption of the Belfast Guidelines on Amnesty and Accountability. This process is relevant both because of its acknowledgement of the need to involve non-lawyers in the formulation of the guidelines and also by adopting guidelines as its format.

Commencing with the latter point, guidelines may be a more appropriate form of developing certain parts of the international law of post-conflict peacebuilding for reasons already referred to directly in Chapter 1 as well as indirectly in Chapter 4 (where the need to avoid rigid approaches in CRP was emphasised). In this context, one may recall that guidelines may eventually develop into permissive rules of international law, allowing the relevant actors latitude to choose which conduct is most conducive to a successful outcome in their specific circumstances. Such an approach is more accommodating to the conflict-specific environment which invariably distinguishes different conflict scenarios. A degree of flexibility may both better meet the specific contexts within which peacebuilding efforts are being made, as well as reduce the perception of formalism, which non-lawyers may find daunting when engaging with fully fledged legal norms.

The Belfast Guidelines' second contribution is that of acknowledging the importance of diverse professional backgrounds when developing principles to be applied in conflict resolution and peacebuilding contexts. The Guidelines state that they were "drafted by an Expert Group of internationally respected human rights and conflict resolution scholars and practitioners".[5] Moreover, the selection of the experts was influenced, inter alia, by what the Guidelines termed "Disciplinary/Professional Expertise" with a view "to bring together leading figures in a range of scholarly and practitioner backgrounds, including law, criminology, psychology and political science". This is a commendable direction and is illustrative of a positive path towards more inclusive processes in the elaboration of international law principles.

However, a more detailed examination of the range of scholars and practitioners included in the elaboration of the Belfast Guidelines still shows a preponderance of legal expertise and academic backgrounds. Out of the 18 members, 11 were professors (or lecturers) in law, while another three were legal professionals. The remaining experts were a professor of peace studies (with an academic background in psychology), a peacebuilding expert (with an academic background in law), another peace practitioner (with an academic background in peace studies) as well a political scientist. This seems to fall short of the multistakeholder approach highlighted above, which calls for an equitable participation in decision-making/shaping processes by those who have an interest in the outcome of the process.

The approach taken in the Belfast Guidelines process is certainly a step in the right direction and it shows that the interaction between legal and non-legal professional backgrounds may yield fruitful results. Nevertheless, a greater involvement of conflict resolution and peace practitioners from outside the legal field would provide a better balance of experiences and perspectives in developing legal principles in post-conflict contexts. The recommendation is to increase the presence of individuals from outside academia and from outside the law.

Another element worth considering is one related to framing. Conflict resolution and peace practice and ethos place substantial emphasis on confidence-building, dialogue, mutual respect, active listening and similar concepts. Bringing together representatives from different groups that have diverse interests and concerns as well as different lived experiences is an important component of conflict resolution.

As evidenced in the previous chapters, the CRP community places a premium on the language and actuality of resolving shared problems through dialogue and problem-solving approaches.[6] Adopting a similar frame in the interaction between actors with legal practitioners and CRP practitioners would possibly be helpful in ensuring a greater engagement from the conflict/peace community. Thus, rather than framing these interactions as Expert Groups, it may be more conducive to frame them as Stakeholder Dialogues (or similar terms). Informality is another hallmark of the collaborative approaches[7] with Mitchell defining interactive conflict resolution as "informal and unofficial processes". References to experts seem not to convey a high degree of informality. Using the terminology of the CRP community is one (albeit limited) way of underlining the genuine collaborative nature of such initiatives, as well as a willingness to adopt the practices and ideas emerging out of CRP. The concept of stakeholder dialogues in shaping the development of the international law of post-conflict peacebuilding is one which could facilitate the involvement of the peace and conflict community along the lines being suggested.

Another initiative that may provide salutary lessons to efforts of adopting a multistakeholder approach to shaping the international law of post-conflict peacebuilding relates to the regulation of private military and security companies (PMSCs) through the Montreux Document. This is a matter which falls more directly within the field of international humanitarian law, although such companies are also often involved in activities in the immediate post-armed conflict phase. The Montreux Document was an initiative undertaken at the behest of the government of Switzerland and the ICRC, with the objective of establishing rules for states in the context of PMSCs. While during the interstate negotiations, academic observers and representatives of PMSCs themselves were present and contributed to the discussion, they were excluded when it came to the final decision-making process. Andrew Clapham who attended the Montreux meetings as an academic observer stated:

> at the last session, when they were actually going to sign the document, those of us, like myself, who were sort of academic observers, but also the private security companies themselves who had been participating in the process up till then, were, I suppose, booted out – would be a way to best explain how the feeling was. So, we were sort of expelled from the room and told that now it was the states who are going to sit amongst themselves.[8]

In the context of shaping international law norm-making, it is important to recall that states still maintain what may be defined as a controlling interest. In the last resort, in the context of the Montreux Document, states considered that the final decisions should be taken autonomously by them and without any input from other actors. In the context of this study, it is valuable to keep in mind that, in practice, governmental structures and interests may be greater obstacles to the effective involvement of the peace and conflict community in shaping law than any reticence on the part of the legal community as a whole. Decision-making in international fora will ultimately remain in the hands of states but it is also an example of errors which genuine multistakeholder approaches should not commit if a process is to be considered by the stakeholders as a genuine one.

The multistakeholder approach being advocated for shaping the field of the international law of peacebuilding is already evident in approaches taken in peacebuilding work itself. The work done by Interpeace is one such example. Interpeace is an organisation devoted to societal capacity-building "to manage conflict in non-violent, non-coercive ways by assisting national actors in their efforts to develop social and political cohesion".[9] They also seek to assist in creating more effective peacebuilding efforts by the international community (especially the UN). They adopt an archetypal peacebuilding approach which emphasises "the wisdom of listening, the power of participation and the strength of informed dialogue to build understanding and trust – the foundations of peacebuilding".[10] This approach, based on consultative and inclusive principles, was abundantly referenced in the previous chapter. Their inclusion in Interpeace's approach is a practical example of the importance of these principles to the CRP community.

The Principles for Peace Initiative, which prior to it becoming an independent Foundation was curated and hosted by Interpeace, is another example of a collaborative, deliberative and consultative approach to peacebuilding. The initiative was created in 2020 through the establishment of an International Commission on Inclusive Peace and a Stakeholder Platform which working together conducted various consultations around the globe. The primary aim of the initiative is to formulate principles for peace-making that advance the work of peacebuilding by connecting the ground realities with overarching strategies with the aim of creating more inclusive and thus more lasting peace processes.

This is very much in line with the aspirations of the nascent international law of post-conflict peacebuilding that lies at the heart of this work. The Principles for Peace Foundation expresses support for a multistakeholder approach through a Stakeholder Platform and emphasises a "collaborative, ecosystem-based approach" while working to expand "a global alliance and new narrative around peace, forming authentic and equitable partnerships through [the] Stakeholder Platform which connects diverse actors for collective action".[11]

However, it is striking that in explaining its work the Foundation states that it offers a new approach to "set standards for peace measurement and serve as an independent convenor, connecting stakeholders across diplomacy, politics, security, and development". Law is absent from this coalition, at least insofar as their stated approach is concerned. This absence is instructive in two ways. Firstly, it fits in with the narrative outlined in Chapter 4 that sees law as being largely outside the purview of the CRP community. Secondly, it underscores the need for the legal community engaged in the normative development of peacebuilding to proactively open spaces for the CRP community within its midst.

The International Commission on Inclusive Peace which led the Foundation's effort to develop its principles for peace was composed of a wide array of highly experienced representatives of the diplomatic, military, conflict resolution, peacebuilding, political, development and UN worlds.[12] However, no member of the Commission had an explicit international law professional background. Once again, as seen with respect to the more law-based initiatives, the disconnect between the CRP and legal communities is very real.

The Foundation has developed 8 principles (in the form of keywords/phrases) thus far: dignity, solidarity, humility, enhancing legitimacy, accountable security, promoting pluralism, adopting subsidiarity, and advocating integrated and hybrid solutions.[13] While these overarching principles are a useful guide to direct the work of peacebuilders both at the macro and micro levels, they could very well be further developed into fully fledged standards that may more efficiently impact the development of the international law of post-conflict peacebuilding.

The expansion of these principles into fully fledged, albeit flexible, guidelines would certainly be assisted by the input of international law practitioners. Their involvement and contribution would also, in itself, assist in moving the principles and would-be guidelines more firmly into the orbit of international law. Such a move would render it more possible and likely that they would shape evolving norms of international law in the context of post-conflict peacebuilding. Without such an interface, the principles and other research conducted or developed by initiatives such as the Principles for Peace Foundation, based on the work of highly experienced practitioners from diverse conflict-related fields, risk being excluded from the debate animating the evolution of the international law of post-conflict peacebuilding.

Possible Future Approaches

Perhaps the most obvious site that may host the multistakeholder approach being advocated is the UN Peacebuilding Commission (PBC), which was mentioned in previous chapters. The PBC by its nature as a UN entity has a certain institutional charisma. It was established jointly by the UN GA and the UN SC in 2005, as an international advisory body with the following mandate which bears citing at some length:

> (a) to bring together all relevant actors to marshal resources and to advise on and propose integrated strategies for post-conflict peacebuilding and recovery; (b) to focus attention on the reconstruction and institution-building efforts necessary for recovery from conflict and to support the development of integrated strategies in order to lay the foundation for sustainable development; and (c) to provide recommendations and information to improve the coordination of all relevant actors within and outside the United Nations, to develop best practices, to help to ensure predictable financing for early recovery activities and to extend the period of attention given by the international community to post-conflict recovery.[14]

The first purpose is precisely to act as a multistakeholder forum for those "relevant actors" involved in "post-conflict peacebuilding and recovery". The second and third purposes include the provision of recommendations on integrated strategies in peacebuilding and on coordination in peacebuilding as well as the development of best practices. All of these seem to fall squarely into the type of 'site profile' being advocated in the context of a multistakeholder forum that may develop guidelines on peacebuilding. However, the PBC has not engaged sufficiently with the type of macro-level work that its mandate seems to imply. Instead, it has primarily focused on supporting specific peacebuilding operations which the UN is involved in. In 2013, Dustin Sharp wrote that "in assessing the PBC's work thus far, its marks for coordination in general have been rather low" and even more pertinently that "[t]he PBC needs to take a stronger leadership role in crafting and proposing creative and integrated solutions to the world's most vexing peacebuilding challenges".[15]

A decade later, the PBC has not moved much -in practice- towards the direction advocated by Sharp. It still focuses most of its limited resources on specific UN peacebuilding mandates. The PBC needs to move away from this approach and instead engage with stakeholders (including, for example, the International Law Commission) to elaborate principles for peacebuilding that may, in time, evolve into a set of wide-ranging peacebuilding guidelines. The PBC has the international profile, the geographic scope and the UN brand that enable it to bring together a range of relevant actors for such a purpose.

Within a regional perspective, another forum which may (and, according to the ethos of this study, should) play a role in developing a productive dialectic of the international law of peacebuilding is the European Union Council Working Party on Public International Law, known in EU jargon as COJUR. COJUR brings together international law experts (usually from the Member States' Foreign Ministries) to discuss and coordinate matters relating to public international law.[16] One of the main aspects of COJUR's work focuses on International Humanitarian Law. In fact, it is tasked with monitoring compliance with the EU guidelines on promoting compliance with international humanitarian which were adopted by the Council of the EU in 2005 (then updated in 2009).[17] COJUR had, in fact, contributed greatly to the development and drafting of these guidelines. Since 2018, COJUR has also published an annual report on compliance in the fulfilment of its mandate.[18] Given that *jus in bello* has featured so prominently in COJUR's work, as has international criminal law (to the extent that a sub-working party on the International Criminal Court was established, which is known as COJUR-ICC), it would seem that a focus on *jus post bellum* would fit in admirably as a complement to COJUR's work.

While COJUR is (and will always be) composed of international law practitioners representing EU Member States, it does engage with NGOs and with experts from outside Foreign Ministries. Indeed, it has become customary for COJUR to invite outside experts to address and interact with the group at each meeting as is customary for COJUR-ICC to hold meetings with NGOs at each of its meetings. This demonstrates that there is no procedural bar on involving more – and more intensely – other experts (including those from non-governmental sectors) in contributing to its work. The main obstacle to this approach related to the willingness of COJUR members to engage with other disciplines and expertise on the basis of equality and within a participatory framework.

COJUR's contribution in this field could be significant. Its experience in International Humanitarian Law and in contributing to the EU guidelines on compliance with IHL makes it a suitable candidate within EU structures to take the initiative for a similar effort in the realm of the international law of post-conflict peacebuilding. Such an initiative would naturally require the approval of the EU Council and coordination with the relevant European Commission directorates such as the Directorate-General for European Civil Protection and Humanitarian Aid and other services both within the Commission and within the European External Action Service. It is well accepted within the EU that the design of policies requires inter-services consultations, and this is in itself an example of professionals from various fields cooperating.

The creation of the EU Maritime Policy in 2009 may serve as an instructive example of the stakeholder approach necessary to create a normative system that is broadly accepted by as large a constituency as possible and that is seen as practicable by those called upon to implement the system on the ground. The approach taken in that case (and in the creation of other EU policies and rules) was fundamentally based on multistakeholder consultations which brought together various Commission services (led by DG MARE but also including Transport, Science, etc.) but also lawyers, scientists such as marine biologists, and representatives of relevant industries (including fisheries and logistics). The European Commissioner responsible for steering through this new policy believes that bringing together all possible stakeholders, and making it clear to them that what they said was really being listened to and internalised, was critical in ensuring that the policy eventually took off.[19] This example from an extraneous field is instructive not only for its multistakeholder approach but also for its adoption of an integrated approach. Prior to its adoption, the EU's policies on maritime affairs were fragmented with distinct and unconnected policies on fisheries, pollution, maritime transport, natural resources, etc. The need for an integrated approach was clear.

This is similar to the various principles, guidelines and norms that inhabit the world of peacebuilding. Demilitarisation, reintegration of combatants, the issue of child soldiers, legitimacy and local ownership, peace education, human rights norms, international criminal procedures, reparations, reconstruction, democratisation are but some of the issues with which we have dealt. And around which a considerable array of principles, guidelines and laws have developed with little to no connection between them. The need to reflect on how the various components of peacebuilding relate to one another and the broader goal of getting closer to positive peace is urgent. This is something which has long been on the CRP agenda. Lederach writing in 1997 set out to encourage practitioners to adopt a more "comprehensive overview of conflict" and to "think about how any given activity and role is related to the long-term goal of sustaining dynamic and constructive processes".[20] Within the legal community, the efforts presented in Chapters 1 and 2 also recognise the need for a comprehensive and integrated normative framework. This is, in fact, the whole *raison d'etre* for creating an international law of post-conflict peacebuilding.

What has not been mentioned, thus far, is the role of academic research initiatives (whether they are theoretical, action oriented or policy oriented) in nurturing the kind of multidisciplinary engagement being advocated. As evidenced in previous chapters, the engagement between international law scholars and CRP scholars remains sub-optimal. This matter needs to be addressed and more joint initiatives should be undertaken within academic and policy fora, with a view to improve understanding and develop a habit of cooperation between disciplines.

As mentioned above, there have been some efforts to develop a multistakeholder approach to dealing with issues relating to post-conflict peacebuilding. What is lacking is a concerted system that: (i) brings together a balanced representation of all relevant stakeholders in the realm of post-conflict peacebuilding including international lawyers, conflict resolution and peacebuilding practitioners, economic specialists, experts in reconstruction and development, etc., (ii) is based on equality of esteem of all participants and a dialogic, participatory decision-making process and (iii) attempts to adopt a holistic view of the entire spectrum of peacebuilding and an integrated approach to shaping the principles, guidelines and norms that govern it.

Conclusion

In conclusion, the engagement of the conflict and peace community with the international law of post-conflict peacebuilding remains a complex and multifaceted challenge. The hesitancy observed amongst some scholars and practitioners in the CRP community to actively participate in legal discussions highlights a prevailing perception that international law is either too specialized or irrelevant to their work. The limited efforts by the legal community to involve the CRP community in the shaping of the international law of post-conflict peacebuilding need strengthening. It is imperative to recognize that the need for increased collaboration between the CRP community and international law is crucial for the effective evolution of norms in post-conflict peacebuilding. For this to happen, appropriate sites for these productive collaborations are required. This chapter has provided some suggestions of sites where these processes may take place.

One of the significant risks in the development of an international law of post-conflict peacebuilding is the potential perception of it being imposed on the peacebuilding sector. To mitigate this risk, a multistakeholder approach is advocated, drawing insights from successful initiatives like the Belfast Guidelines on Amnesty and Accountability. The guidelines, developed with the involvement of non-lawyers, suggest that guidelines may be a more suitable format for certain aspects of international law in post-conflict settings. This approach allows for flexibility, accommodating diverse conflict scenarios and reducing the perceived formalism that may hinder non-lawyers' engagement with legal norms.

However, a closer examination of initiatives like the Belfast Guidelines reveals a predominant presence of legal expertise amongst the experts involved. To enhance inclusivity and balance, there is a recommendation to increase the involvement of conflict resolution and peace practitioners from outside the legal field. Framing interactions as Stakeholder Dialogues rather than Expert Groups might better align with the ethos of conflict resolution, emphasizing concepts such as confidence-building, dialogue and mutual respect.

Drawing lessons from initiatives such as the Montreux Document on PMSCs, it becomes evident that the involvement of non-state actors in shaping legal norms can face challenges. In the context of post-conflict peacebuilding, governmental structures and interests may pose significant obstacles to effective engagement with the peace and conflict community. The Principles for Peace Foundation, while emphasizing multistakeholder collaboration, lacks explicit representation from international law backgrounds. While the foundation's principles serve as a useful guide, their expansion into flexible guidelines could benefit from the input of international law practitioners, facilitating their integration into the evolving norms of international law in post-conflict peacebuilding.

The European Union Council Working Party on Public International Law (COJUR) stands out as a potential forum for a productive dialectic on the international law of peacebuilding. COJUR's experience in international humanitarian law provides an interesting insight. A substantially increased engagement with experts from outside Foreign Ministries and a willingness to involve more actively non-state actors in their work would be positive steps in this regard. A concerted effort would be needed within COJUR to ensure a more inclusive approach that considers diverse perspectives, including those from conflict resolution and peacebuilding practitioners.

Within the UN system, the PBC appears, *prima facie*, as the ideal site for a multistakeholder process with a view to developing a comprehensive and integrated approach to the governance of post-conflict peacebuilding. It has, however, not been able or willing to take on such a role. The reasons for such reticence need to be explored and addressed. Its traditional role of providing ad hoc recommendations for UN peacebuilding missions does not reflect adequately its original mandate nor does it contribute to take forward the peacebuilding agenda as a whole.

In summary, developing a comprehensive and inclusive international law of post-conflict peacebuilding requires a concerted effort to bridge the gap between legal experts and practitioners from the CRP community. A multistakeholder approach, framed as Stakeholder Dialogues, and drawing lessons from successful initiatives, can pave the way for a more collaborative and effective evolution of norms in this critical area. The challenge lies not only in overcoming hesitancy within the CRP community but also in addressing institutional and governmental obstacles to meaningful engagement. Only through such collaborative efforts can the evolving international law of post-conflict peacebuilding truly meet the diverse and dynamic challenges faced by those working on the ground for positive peace.

Notes

1 Interview with BIN, in discussion with author, Sarajevo, 8 March 2023.
2 Interview with Professor Brice Dickson, online discussion with author, 24 August 2023.
3 Dodds, F. (2002). The Context: Multistakeholder and Global Governance. In *Multi Stakeholder Processes for Governance and Sustainability: Beyond Deadlock and Conflict,* ed. Hermatti, M., 28. Earthscan.
4 United Nations. (1998). Statement by Kofi Annan, Secretary General of the United Nations to the World Economic Forum, 31 January 1998. https://press.un.org/en/1998/19980130.sgsm6448.html (accessed June 8, 2024).
5 Transitional Justice Institute. (2013). Belfast Guidelines on Amnesty and Accountability, Transitional Justice Institute at the University of Ulster. https://www.ulster.ac.uk/__data/assets/pdf_file/0005/57839/TheBelfastGuidelinesFINAL_000.pdf (accessed June 8, 2024).
6 In this context John Paul Lederach refers to problem-solving workshops as being based on collaborative analysis and viewing the conflict as a shared problem. The emphasis in such settings is on relational issues, collaboration and sharing rather than on technical expertise. Lederach, J. P. (1998). *Building Peace: Sustainable Reconciliation in Divided Societies*. United States Institute for Peace Press: 46.
7 Mitchell, C. (2001). From Controlled Communication to Problem Solving: The Origins of Facilitated Conflict Resolution. *The International Journal of Peace Studies* 6 (1). https://www3.gmu.edu/programs/icar/ijps/vol6_1/Mitchell2.htm
8 The Responsible Security Association. (2023). Interview with Andrew Clapham. https://blog.icoca.ch/international-code-of-conduct/ (accessed June 6, 2024).
9 See Interpeace Missions and Values. Mission & Values. https://www.interpeace.org/who-we-are/mission-and-values/ (accessed June 10, 2024).
10 International Organization for Peacebuilding. Mission & Values. https://www.interpeace.org/who-we-are/mission-and-values/ (accessed June 8, 2024).
11 See Principle for Peace. Advancing Peace Processes. https://principlesforpeace.org/what-we-do/ (accessed June 18, 2024).
12 See the composition of the International Commission for Inclusive Peace at Interpeace. Re-Shaping Peace Processes. https://www.interpeace.org/2020/12/press-release-reshaping-peace-processes/ (accessed June 10, 2024).
13 Principles for Peace. https://principlesforpeace.org/the-principles/ (accessed June 8, 2024)
14 United Nations Security Council Resolution 1645, 20 December 2005, S/RES/1645 (2005).
15 Sharp, D. Bridging the Gap: The United Nations Peacebuilding Commission and the Challenges of Integrating DDR and Transitional Justice. In *Transitional Justice and Peacebuilding on the Ground*, eds Sriram, C. et al. New York: Routledge: 37.
16 Council of the European Union. Council Working Party on Public International Law. https://www.consilium.europa.eu/en/council-eu/preparatory-bodies/working-party-public-international-law/ (accessed June 10, 2024).
17 European Union. (2018). EU Guidelines on Promoting Compliance with International Humanitarian Law (IHL). https://www.eeas.europa.eu/sites/default/files/04_hr_guidelines_humanitarian_en_0.pdf (accessed June 10, 2024).

18 European Union. (2022). Report on the EU guidelines on promoting compliance with international humanitarian law. https://www.consilium.europa.eu/media/59995/2022_456_ihl-report_en_04_web-final.pdf (accessed June 10, 2024).
19 Interview with Dr Joe Borg (former European Commissioner for Fisheries and Maritime Affairs), in discussion with author, Malta, 9 May 2023.
20 Lederach, J. P., *Building Peace*: 71.

6 Conclusion

This study has demonstrated that in post-conflict peacebuilding, several legal scholars are on a tentative quest to shape the development of a *jus pacis post bellum*. Presumably, this stems from the belief that the role of international law is important in shaping the contours of a just and sustainable peace.

The ensuing corpus of academic work is impressive in so far as legal scholarship is concerned. However, it is also remarkable that it does not feature and factor in insights and perspectives of CRP scholars. Existing legal scholarship also underlines the fact that there is still substantial work to be done in order to formulate a legal framework of the international law of post-conflict peacebuilding. In this context, the exact scope of the application and its precise legal content have not yet crystallised. Chapter 2 provided insights as to the extent of the "work in progress" nature of this area of international law.

A legal framework that is still "in formation" presents opportunities to include a wider range of voices in its shaping. However, for this to happen, lawyers and non-lawyers in CRP need to collaborate and cross-fertilise their respective disciplines. CRP has always been a melting pot of disciplines and approaches, and accordingly, the CRP community should welcome such a deeper interaction with the legal community.

This far, this interaction has been rather limited. Law has traditionally been a more self-contained discipline with the exceptions of philosophy and theology with which it has always had strong connections. Lawyers, generally, are seen to be less keen on involving other disciplines with their profession. Several reasons for this relative lack of proactive collaboration between lawyers and non-lawyers within CRP are adumbrated in Chapter 3. Increasing such proactive collaboration between lawyers and non-lawyers generally would facilitate the framework of post-conflict peacebuilding.

The following chapters have sought to evidence that the creation and implementation of the international law of post-conflict peacebuilding should not be confined to the realm of legal experts alone. The fundamental premise for this statement is that any normative framework governing the post-conflict setting will impact directly conflict resolution and peacebuilding practitioners. Moreover, while lawyers working on the international law of peacebuilding possess

DOI: 10.4324/9781003462248-6

considerable technical knowledge on the subject, other professionals within CRP, such as conflict analysts, diplomats, mediators, social psychologists, anthropologists, engineers and sociologists, just to mention a few, possess knowledge and expertise on a number of important issues. These include issues like confidence-building measures, reconciliation methods, reconstruction requirements, local governance, community relations, timings of transition, etc.

Legal frameworks through peace agreements or other forms of transitional agreements are important in creating some kind of regulatory or governance system within a post-conflict setting. The technical dimension of drafting such agreements and casting them in appropriate legal form is clearly a matter for lawyers. However, the inclusion of a diverse array of conflict resolution and peace practitioners is equally important to render such agreements more resilient. In exploring this paradigm shift, what emerges clearly is the need for legal expertise to intertwine with the insights of practitioners from various disciplines, fostering a more comprehensive and adaptable foundation for lasting peace.

The brief exploration of some of the principles and approaches developed by the scholars and practitioners within the CRP community in Chapter 4 is certainly not exhaustive. However, even the limited selection of principles and approaches presented illustrates the multifaceted nature of post-conflict peacebuilding. The principles discussed in Chapter 4 evidence that the challenges of peacebuilding extend beyond the purview of legal intricacies. Peacebuilding is not a linear process nor, I would contend, is it a primarily legal one. While legal frameworks assist in moving the peacebuilding processes, the perceptions of the relevant stakeholders, the willingness of the parties to compromise, the quality of leadership of the parties and numerous other factors all impact on the success and sustainability (or otherwise) of peacebuilding. Thus, its success relies on a multidimensional understanding of the complexities that underlie conflicts and the subsequent transition to peace.

To broaden our perspective, we must recognise the invaluable contributions of conflict resolution and peace practitioners who study conflict and peace extensively and who operate on the ground, navigating the tangled web of societal dynamics, cultural nuances and human experiences. These scholars and practitioners possess a wealth of experiential knowledge that may complement and enhance the content of the legal foundations laid down by international law. The issues addressed in Chapter 4, apart from not being comprehensive, were also presented as interrogations rather than answers. The hope is that further reflection and research on the intersection between the international law of post-conflict peacebuilding and the CRP principles and approaches presented (and, no doubt, many others) will be undertaken going forward.

In the pursuit of positive peace, we must bridge the gap between legal doctrine and on-the-ground realities, acknowledging that the dynamics of post-conflict societies are living entities that demand adaptive and nuanced approaches rather than overly rigid structures. The recommendations relating to the formulation of permissive international law norms, initially framed as guidelines that provide scope for negotiation to the stakeholders would be a useful step in this direction. One of the key principles that permeates CRP thinking is that in resolving conflicts and building peace cannot rely on rigid structures; instead, we need to have governance structures that move peacebuilding processes forward acknowledging the primacy of local conditions. It is suggested that most of the framework of the international law of post-conflict peacebuilding should take the form of guidelines and permissive rules of law. Certain basic principles may be adopted as mandatory given their overarching nature in post-conflict situations. Two general principles that, in light of the insights arising out of the CRP community, should be established as mandatory rules of international law are those calling for local ownership and inclusivity in peacebuilding.

While the above reflections argue for the inclusion of non-legal expertise, one should also focus on equally important considerations as to how such an inclusionary approach may best be achieved. Chapter 5 calls for the explicit adoption of a multistakeholder approach.

In making such a call, sites where such a multistakeholder engagement has been made are referred to and other sites where such approaches should be adopted are recommended. However, even when considering the example of various fora which could be suitable to host such interaction, one noted the predominance of international lawyers even when other professional backgrounds were included. A more balanced representation of legal expertise and conflict resolution/peacebuilding expertise needs to be actively sought and achieved in the relevant.

Instances from other areas of governance that are pertinent to international law, such as maritime governance and internet governance, are offered as experiences to reflect upon. One site which seems an obvious candidate to undertake such an intersectional role is the PBC. It is pertinent to note that whatever its contribution to strengthening individual UN peacebuilding missions, it has largely failed to take the lead in formulating integrative and comprehensive peacebuilding principles with input from a wide array of geographic, disciplinary and gender perspectives. The reasons for this shortcoming merit further examination and possibilities for progress explored.

In essence, the primary questions this study sought to answer are

- i Whether the international law of post-conflict peacebuilding should involve CRP scholars and practitioners?
- ii What kind of contribution could the CRP community make to the international law of post-conflict peacebuilding?
- iii What sites may be conducive to a greater involvement of the CRP community with international law?

Regarding question (i), the need to involve the CRP community in shaping the international law of peacebuilding appears clear and the time for doing so is propitious.

In terms of the second question, one may submit that the contribution of the CRP community would provide a different lens through which to view the role, scope and content of the international law of post-conflict peacebuilding. Since its inception in the 1960s and its fast evolution in the 1980s and 1990s, the CRP community has evolved a number of principles and promulgated approaches which assist in identifying the nature of violent conflict and the ways in which such conflict may transformed into positive peace.

The few examples of such principles and approaches identified in Chapter 4 suffice to illustrate the range and nature of the contribution which the CRP community may make towards the formulation of a normative peacebuilding framework. The focus within CRP on structural and cultural violence with the attendant emphasis on the relevance of transforming structures (within the international community and domestic communities) is a key example of a perspective that may guide the shaping of this branch of international law. The issues of phasing, priorities and time-frames which CRP scholar-practitioners have grappled with is another such example, which may be particularly useful in balancing the "peace v justice" conundrum, which has for so long bedevilled the relationship between lawyers and peacebuilders.

The third question related to sites where such interaction between the legal community and the CRP community may take place. Suggestions were made in Chapter 5 along the lines mentioned above. However, beyond these types of institutional or semi-institutional sites, there are also informal, unofficial and more flexible loci for cooperation. In particular, an increased participation of CRP specialists and international law scholars and practitioners in collaborative projects would also be a step in the right direction. Such projects may consist of both shared research agendas as well as the design of conflict resolution and peacebuilding interventions. These types of joint initiatives would foster a greater collaborative sense between the two disciplines. They would also help all of us involved in this sector recognize that international law may be a crucial (and not peripheral aspect of peacebuilding) and that the expertise developed by the CRP community is an essential component in shaping the nascent field of the international law of post-conflict peacebuilding.

Finally, this study has sought to analyse the current existing frameworks, both legal and theoretical, while simultaneously attempting to demonstrate why there is an urgent necessity to push the boundaries and challenge the status quo. In reacting to current realities, it has attempted to trace a path to future solutions, by setting some markers and stimulating a constructive debate that will one day make *jus pacis post bellum* easier to define and implement in practice.

Bibliography

Judicial Decisions

Accordance with International Law of the Unilateral Declaration of Independence in Respect of Kosovo (Request for Advisory Opinion), CGJ 423 (ICJ 2010), 22nd July 2010, International Court of Justice (ICJ).

Azanian People's Organization (AZAPO) v President of the Republic of South Africa, 25 July 1996, CCT17/96, ZACC 16.

Continental Shelf Case (*Tunisia v Libyan Arab Jamahiriya*) ICGJ 126 (ICJ 1982), 24th February 1982, International Court of Justice (ICJ)

The Case of S.S. Lotus (France v. Turkey) ICGJ 248 (PCIJ 1927) 7th September 1927, Permanent Court of International Justice (PCIJ).

Conventions

Charter of the International Military Tribunal – Annex to the Agreement for the prosecution and punishment of the major war criminals of the European Axis, United Nations, 8 August 1945 (entered into force 8 August 1945)

International Covenant on Economic, Social and Cultural Rights, 16 December 1966, (entered into force 3 January 1976).

Statute of the International Criminal Court, 17 July 1998 (entered into force 1 July 2002).

Statute of the International Court of Justice, 26 June 1945, (entered into force October 24, 1945).

United Nations Convention on the Rights of the Child, 20 November 1989, (entered into force 2 September 1990).

Vienna Convention on the Law of the Treaties, 23 May 1969, Vol. 1155 (entered into force 27 January 1980).

General Reports and Studies

European Union. (2018). EU Guidelines on Promoting Compliance with International Humanitarian Law (IHL). https://www.eeas.europa.eu/sites/default/files/04_hr_guidelines_humanitarian_en_0.pdf (accessed June 10, 2024).

European Union. (2022). Report on the EU Guidelines on Promoting Compliance with International Humanitarian Law. https://www.consilium.europa.eu/media/59995/2022_456_ihl-report_en_04_web-final.pdf (accessed June 10, 2024).

International Committee of the Red Cross. (2011). How Does Law Protect in War? Fundamental Principles of IHL. https://casebook.icrc.org/law/fundamentals-ihl (accessed February 13, 2023).

Report of the Secretary General Pursuant to the Statement Adopted at the Summit Meeting of the Security Council on 31 January 1992. 17 June 1992. SC Doc. S/24111. https://www.securitycouncilreport.org/atf/cf/%7B65BFCF9B-6D27-4E9C-8CD3-CF6E4FF96FF9%7D/Disarm%20S24111.pdf

Transitional Justice Institute. (2013). Belfast Guidelines on Amnesty and Accountability, Transitional Justice Institute at the University of Ulster. https://www.ulster.ac.uk/__data/assets/pdf_file/0005/57839/TheBelfastGuidelinesFINAL_000.pdf (accessed June 8, 2024).

United Nations. (2010). UN Peacebuilding: An Orientation. https://www.un.org/peacebuilding/sites/www.un.org.peacebuilding/files/documents/peacebuilding_orientation.pdf (accessed June 8, 2024).

Interviews

Interview with Dr. Joe Borg, in discussion with author, Malta, 9 May 2023.

Interview with Professor Brice Dickson, online discussion with author, 24 August 2023.

Interview with Professor Pamina Firchow, online discussion with author, 21 August 2023.

Interview with Professor Midhat Izmirlija, in discussion with the author, Sarajevo, Bosnia and Herzegovina, 8 March 2023.

Interview with an official of the Office of the High Representative for Bosnia Herzegovina, online discussion with the author, 17 March 2023.

Interview with an official of the Office of the Ombudsperson, Sarajevo, Bosnia Herzegovina, in discussion with the author, Sarajevo, Bosnia and Herzegovina, 8 March 2023.

Interview with representatives of the Network for Peacebuilding in discussion with the author, Sarajevo, Bosnia and Herzegovina, 7 March 2023.

Interview with representatives of the Balkan Investigative Network, in discussion with the author, Sarajevo, Bosnia and Herzegovina, 8 March 2023.

Interview with an official with the Ministry of Foreign Affairs of the Republic of Cyprus, in discussion with the author, Nicosia, Cyprus, 2 October 2022.

United Nations Documents

Accordance with international law of the unilateral declaration of independence in respect of Kosovo, International Court of Justice, 22 July 2010.

Resolution adopted by the General Assembly on Strengthening the role of mediation in the peaceful settlement of disputes, conflict prevention and resolution, 9 September 2016, A/RES/70/304.

Resolution adopted by the General Assembly on Strengthening the role of mediation in the peaceful settlement of disputes, conflict prevention and resolution, 28 July 2011, A/RES/65/283

United Nations DDR Integrated Disarmament, Demobilization and Reintegration Standards (IDDRS). (2006). (last updated 2019) https://www.unddr.org/operational-guide-iddrs/ (accessed February 13, 2023).

United Nations. (1993). Vienna Declaration and Programme of Action adopted by the World Conference on Human Rights in Vienna on 25 June 1993.

United Nations. (1996). Report of the Fourth World Conference on Women, Beijing, 4–15 September 1995. https://www.un.org/womenwatch/daw/beijing/pdf/Beijing%20full%20report%20E.pdf

United Nations. (1998). Statement by Kofi Annan, Secretary General of the United Nations to the World Economic Forum, 31 January 1998. https://press.un.org/en/1998/19980130.sgsm6448.html (accessed June 8, 2024).

United Nations. (2004). Letter Dated 15 September 1989 from the Permanent Representative of Trinidad and Tobago to the United Nations President of the General Assembly. https://digitallibrary.un.org/record/73974?ln=zh_CN (accessed on February 13, 2023).

United Nations Security Council Resolution 1645, 20 December 2005, S/RES/1645 (2005).

United Nations Security Council Resolution 1325, 31 October 2000, S/RES/1325 (2000).

United Nations Set of principles for the protection and promotion of human rights through action to combat impunity, 1997, E/CN.4/Sub.2/1997/20/Rev.1 (updated in 2005).

Books

Annan, Kofi. (2000). *We the Peoples: The Role of the United Nations in the 21st Century*. New York: United Nations.

Bell, Christine. (2003). *Human Rights and Peace Agreement*. Oxford: Oxford University Press.

Bingham, Tom. (2011). *The Rule of Law*. New York: Penguin Books.

Boutros-Ghali, Boutros. (1992). *An Agenda for Peace: Preventive Diplomacy, Peacemaking and Peace-Keeping*. United Nations

Burton, John. (1990). *Conflict: Human Needs Theory*. London: Palgrave Macmillan.

Chetail, Vincent. (2009). *Post-Conflict Peacebuilding: A Lexicon*. Oxford: Oxford University Press.

Coleman, Peter T., Deutsch, Morton, and Marcus, Eric C. (2014). *The Handbook of Conflict Resolution: Theory and Practice* (3rd edition). New Jersey: Jossey Bass.

Deutsch, Morton. (1985). *Distributive Justice: A Social-Psychological Perspective*. New Haven: Yale University Press.

Dickson, Brice. (2012). *The European Convention on Human Rights and the Conflict in Northern Ireland*. Oxford: Oxford University Press.

Donais, Timothy. (2012). *Peacebuilding and Local Ownership: Post-Conflict Consensus-Building*. Oxon: Routledge.

Fisher, Roger, Ury, William, and Patton, Bruce. (1991). *Getting to Yes: Negotiating Agreement without Giving In*. New York: Penguin Books.

Fisher, Ronald and Herbert, Kelman. (2003). *Conflict Analysis and Resolution*. Oxford: Oxford University Press.

Gaeta, Paola, Visuals, Jorge E., and Zappalá, Salvatore. (2020). *Cassese's International Law*. Oxford: Oxford University Press.

Goodale, Mark. (2022). *Reinventing Human Rights*. California: Stanford University Press.

Grech, Omar. (2017). *Human Rights and the Northern Ireland Conflict*. New York: Routledge.

Hinton, Alexander L. (2011). *Transitional Justice: Global Mechanisms and Local Realities After Genocide and Mass Violence*. New Brunswick: Rutgers University Press.

Hirsch, Susan F. and Paczyńska, Agnieszka. (2024). *Teaching Peace and Conflict Studies: Engaged Learning and Inclusive Theory*. Cheltenham: Edward Elgar Publishing.

Irvin-Erickson, Douglas. (2016). *Raphaël Lemkin and the Concept of Genocide*. Philadelphia: University of Pennsylvania Press.

Lawther, Cheryl and Moffett, Luke. (2023). *Research Handbook on Transitional Justice*. Cheltenham: Edward Elgar Publishing.

Lederach, John Paul. (1998). *Building Peace: Sustainable Reconciliation in Divided Societies*. Washington: United States Institute for Peace Press.

Minow, Martha. (1999). *Between Vengeance and Forgiveness: Facing History after Genocide and Mass Violence*. Boston: Beacon Press.

Mitchell. Christopher. (2014). *The Nature of Intractable Conflict: Resolution in the Twenty-First Century*. London: Palgrave Macmillan

Mitchell, Christopher R. and Hancock, Landon E. (2012). *Local Peacebuilding and National Peace: Interaction between Grassroots and Elite Processes*. New York: Bloomsbury Publishing.

Moore, Christopher W. (2014). *The Mediation Process: Practical Strategies for Resolving Conflict* (4th edition). New Jersey: Jossey-Bass.

Ramsbotham, Oliver, Woodhouse, Tom, and Miall, Hugh. (2016). *Contemporary Conflict Resolution* (4th edition). Cambridge: Polity.

Roberti di Sarsina, Jacopo. (2019). *Transitional Justice and a State's Response to Mass Atrocity*. Berlin: Springer.

Rubenstein, Richard E. (2017). *Resolving Structural Conflicts*. Oxford: Routledge.

Stahn, Carsten and Iverson, Jens. (2020). *Just Peace After Conflict: Jus Post Bellum and the Justice of Peace*. Oxford: Oxford University Press.

Stahn, Carsten, Easterday, Jennifer S. and Iverson, Jens. (2014). *Jus Post Bellum: Mapping the Normative Functions*. Oxford: Oxford University Press.

Taylor, A. J. P. (1961). *The Origins of the Second World War*. London: Hamish Hamilton.

Tonge, Jonathan. (2002). *Northern Ireland: Conflict and Change* (2nd edition). New York: Routledge.

Book Chapters

Atashi, Elham. (2009). Challenges to Conflict Transformation from the Streets. In *Conflict Transformation and Peacebuilding*, eds Dayton, Bruce W. and Kriesberg, Louis. London: Routledge.

Bartoli, Andrea., Civico, Aldo, and Gianturco, Leone. (2009). Mozambique-Renamo. In *Conflict Transformation and Peacebuilding*, eds Dayton, Bruce W. and Kriesberg, Louis. London: Routledge.

Dodds, Felix. (2002). The Context: Multistakeholder and Global Governance. In *Multi Stakeholder Processes for Governance and Sustainability: Beyond Deadlock and Conflict*, ed. Hermatti, Minu, 28. Earthscan.

English, Michael D. and Rubenstein, Richard E. (2022). Systemic Violence. In *Encyclopedia of Violence, Peace, & Conflict* (3rd edition), ed. Kurtz, Lester. Oxford: Academic Press.

Falk, Richard. (2022). International Law. In *Encyclopedia of Violence, Peace, & Conflict* (3rd edition), ed. Kurtz, Lester. Oxford: Academic Press

Grech, Omar. (2010). Human Rights and the Conflict Cycle: A Synopsis. In *Human Rights and the Conflict Cycle*, eds Grech, Omar and Wohlfeld, Monika. Msida: MEDAC.

Jabri, Vivienne. (2016). Post-Colonialism: A Post-Colonial Perspective on Peacebuilding. In *The Palgrave Handbook of Disciplinary and Regional Approaches to Peace*, eds Richmond, Oliver P., Pogodda, Sandra, and Ramović, Jasmin. New York: Palgrave Macmillan

Lambourne, Wendy. (2006). Justice in the Aftermath of Mass Crimes: International Law and Peacebuilding. In *The Challenge of Conflict: International Law Responds*, eds Ustina Dolgopol and Gardma, Judith. Leiden: Brill.

Lyons, Terrence. (2009). Peacebuilding, Democratization, and Transforming the Institutions of War. In *Conflict Transformation and Peacebuilding*, eds Dayton, Bruce W. and Kriesberg, Louis. London: Routledge.

Mac Ginty, Roger. (2006). Northern Ireland: A Peace Process Thwarted by Accidental Spoiling. In *Challenges to Peacebuilding: Managing Spoilers During Conflict Resolution*, eds Newman, Edward and Richmond, Oliver. Tokyo: UNU Press

Sharp, Dustin. (2013). Bridging the Gap: The United Nations Peacebuilding Commission and the Challenges of Integrating DDR and Transitional Justice. In *Transitional Justice and Peacebuilding on the Ground*, eds Sriram, Chandra et al., New York: Routledge.

Journal Articles

Añaños, M. Cecilia. (2011). La consolidación de la paz en el derecho internacional. *Estudios Internacionales* 168, 51–86.

Anonymous. (1996). Human Rights and Conflict. *Human Rights Quarterly* 18 (2), 249–258.

Berdal, Mats and Ucko David H. (2013). Introduction to the DDR Forum: Rethinking the Reintegration of Former Combatants. *International Peacekeeping* 20 (3), 316–320.

Charlesworth, Hilary. (2007). Law after War, *Melbourne Journal of International Law* 8 (2), 233–247.

Chinkin, Christine and Charlesworth, Hilary. (2006). Building Women into Peace: The International Legal Framework. *Third World Quarterly* 27. 937–957

Elkins, James R. (1996). Thinking Like a Lawyer: Second Thoughts. *Mercer Law Review* 47 (2). 511–541

Gizelis, Theodora Ismene. (2011). A Country of Their Own. Women and Peacebuilding. *Conflict Management and Peace Science* 28 (5), 522–542.

Hilpold, Peter. (2015). Jus Post Bellum and the Responsibility to Rebuild – Identifying the Contours of an Ever More Important Aspect of R2P. *Journal of International Humanitarian Legal Studies* 6, 284–305.

Kaplan, Oliver and Nussio, Enzo. (2018). Community Counts: The Social Reintegration of Ex-Combatants in Colombia. *Conflict Management and Peace Science* 35 (2), 132–153.

King, Elisabeth and Matthews, Robert O. (2012). A New Agenda for Peace: 20 Years Later. *International Journal* 64 (2), 275–293. https://www.jstor.org/stable/23266007

Ladipoth, Ruth. (2017). Equity in International Law, Proceedings of the Annual Meeting. *American Society of International Law* 81, 138–147.

Mitchell Christopher. (2001). From Controlled Communication to Problem Solving: The Origins of Facilitated Conflict Resolution. *The International Journal of Peace Studies* 6 (1). https://www3.gmu.edu/programs/icar/ijps/vol6_1/Mitchell2.htm

Nolan-Haley, Jacqueline. (2002). Lawyers, Non-Lawyers and Mediation: Rethinking the Professional Monopoly from a Problem-Solving Perspective. *Harvard Negotiation Law Review* 235–299.

Oeter, Stefan. (2005). *Post-Conflict Peacebuilding – Völkerrechtliche Aspekte der Friedenskonsolidierung in Nachkriegsgesellschaften. Die Friedens-Warte* 80.

Rolston, Bill. (2007). Demobilization and Reintegration of Ex-Combatants: The Irish Case in International Perspective. *Social and Legal Studies* 16 (2), 259–280.

Rubenstein Richard E. and Bleckman Frank O. (1999). Conflict Resolution and Distributive Justice: Reflections on the Burton Laue-Debate. *Peace and Conflict Studies* 6 (1). https://nsuworks.nova.edu/cgi/viewcontent.cgi?article=1198&context=pcs

Stahn, Carsten. (2006). 'Jus ad bellum', 'jus in bello'…'jus post bellum?' – Rethinking the Conception of the Law of Armed Force. *European Journal of International Law* 17 (5) 921–943.

Welch, Claude E. Jr. and Watkins, Ashley F. (2011). Extending Enforcement: The Coalition for the International Criminal Court. *Human Rights Quarterly* 30, 928.

Websites

Coalition for the International Criminal Court. Our Story, the Coalition for the International Criminal Court. https://www.coalitionfortheicc.org/node/1072 (accessed February 13, 2023).

Council of the European Union. (2024). Council Working Party on Public International Law. https://www.consilium.europa.eu/en/council-eu/preparatory-bodies/working-party-public-international-law/ (accessed June 10, 2024).

International Organization for Peacebuilding. Mission & Values. https://www.interpeace.org/who-we-are/mission-and-values/ (accessed June 8, 2024).

International Commission for Inclusive Peace at Interpeace. (2020). Re-Shaping Peace Processes. https://www.interpeace.org/2020/12/press-release-reshaping-peace-processes/ (accessed June 10, 2024).

Interpeace Missions and Values. Mission & Values. https://www.interpeace.org/who-we-are/mission-and-values/ (accessed June 10, 2024).

Katz, Neil and McNulty, Kevin. (1994). *Conflict Resolution.* Maxwell School of Citizenship and Public Affairs. https://www.maxwell.syr.edu/docs/default-source/ektron-files/conflict-resolution-neil-katz-and-kevin-mcnulty.pdf?sfvrsn=4de5d71e_9 (accessed June 6, 2024).

McCrudden, Christopher. (2018). Twenty Years on from the Good Friday Agreement. The British Academy Blog. https://www.thebritishacademy.ac.uk/blog/twenty-years-good-friday-agreement/

Principles for Peace. Advancing Peace Processes. https://principlesforpeace.org/what-we-do/ (accessed June 18, 2024).

The Responsible Security Association. (2023). Interview with Andrew Clapham. https://blog.icoca.ch/international-code-of-conduct/ (accessed June 6, 2024).

UNESCO. 2023. What You Need to Know About UNESCO's Recommendation on Education for Peace, Human Rights and Sustainable Development. https://www.unesco.org/en/articles/what-you-need-know-about-unescos-recommendation-education-peace-human-rights-and-sustainable (accessed May 28, 2024).

United Nations. 2023. Replica of Peace Treaty Between Hattusilis and Ramses II. https://www.un.org/ungifts/replica-peace-treaty-between-hattusilis-and-ramses-ii#:~:text=This%20Kadesh%20Peace%20Treaty%20is,Ramses%2C%20Pharaoh%20of%20the%20Egyptians (accessed February 13, 2023).

United Nations Peace Maker. Group of Friends of Mediation. https://peacemaker.un.org/networks/group-of-friends

Occasional Papers

Chetail, Vincent and Jütersonke, Oliver. (2015). Peacebuilding: A Review of the Academic Literature. Geneva Peacebuilding Platform. White Paper Series No.13.

Nitter, James and Diamond, Louise. (1996). Building Peace and Transforming Conflict: Multi-Track Diplomacy in Practice. The Institute for Multi-Track Diplomacy: Occasional Paper Number 7.

Schaller, Christian. (2009). Towards an International Legal Framework for Post-Conflict Peacebuilding, SWP Research Paper, RP 3 (February): 5. https://www.swp-berlin.org/publications/products/research_papers/2009_RP03_slr_ks.pdf

Index

Note: Page references with "n" denote endnotes.

For Product Safety Concerns and Information please contact our EU representative GPSR@taylorandfrancis.com
Taylor & Francis Verlag GmbH, Kaufingerstraße 24, 80331 München, Germany

www.ingramcontent.com/pod-product-compliance
Lightning Source LLC
LaVergne TN
LVHW010935110826
845149LV00013B/2617